the archy and mehitabel omnibus

the archy and mehitabel
omnibus

archy and mehitabel
with
archy's life of mehitabel
by
don marquis

faber and faber

first published in omnibus form in 1998
by faber and faber limited
3 queen square london wc1n 3au

archy and mehitabel
first published by ernest benn in 1931
published by faber and faber in 1934
faber paperback edition 1958

archy's life of mehitabel
first published by faber and faber in 1934
faber paperback edition 1961

photoset by avon dataset ltd, bidford on avon
printed and bound in great britain by
mackays of chatham plc, chatham, kent

a cip record for this book
is available from the british library

isbn 0 571 19386 2

2 4 6 8 10 9 7 5 3 1

contents

archy and mehitabel

dedicated to babs
with babs knows what
and babs knows why

acknowledgment

the author is indebted to the proprietors of the new york sun, the new york herald-tribune, and p.f. collier and son company for permission to reprint these sketches

contents

5

the coming of archy

The circumstances of Archy's first appearance are narrated in the following extract from the Sun Dial column of the New York *Sun*.

Dobbs Ferry possesses a rat which slips out of his lair at night and runs a typewriting machine in a garage. Unfortunately, he has always been interrupted by the watchman before he could produce a complete story.

It was at first thought that the power which made the typewriter run was a ghost, instead of a rat. It seems likely to us that it was both a ghost and a rat. Mme Blavatsky's ego went into a white horse after she passed over, and someone's personality has undoubtedly gone into this rat. It is an era of belief in communications from the spirit land.

And since this matter had been reported in the public prints and seriously received we are no longer afraid of being ridiculed, and we do not mind making a statement of something that happened to our own typewriter only a couple of weeks ago.

We came into our room earlier than usual in the morning, and discovered a gigantic cockroach jumping about upon the keys.

He did not see us, and we watched him. He would climb painfully upon the framework of the machine and cast himself with all his force upon a key, head downward, and his weight and the impact of the blow were just sufficient to operate the machine, one slow letter after another. He could not work the capital letters, and he had a great deal of difficulty operating the mechanism that shifts the paper so that a fresh line may be started. We never saw a cockroach work so hard or perspire so freely in all our lives before. After about an hour of this frightfully difficult literary labour he fell to the floor exhausted, and we saw him creep feebly into a nest of the poems which are always there in profusion.

Congratulating ourself that we had left a sheet of paper in the machine the night before so that all this work had not been in vain, we made an examination, and this is what we found:

expression is the need of my soul
i was once a vers libre bard
but i died and my soul went into the body of a cockroach
it has given me a new outlook upon life
i see things from the under side now
thank you for the apple peelings in the wastepaper basket
but your paste is getting so stale i cant eat it
there is a cat here called mehitabel i wish you would have
removed she nearly ate me the other night why dont she
catch rats that is what she is supposed to be for
there is a rat here she should get without delay

most of these rats here are just rats
but this rat is like me he has a human soul in him
he used to be a poet himself
night after night i have written poetry for you
on your typewriter
and this big brute of a rat who used to be a poet
comes out of his hole when it is done
and reads it and sniffs at it

8

he is jealous of my poetry
he used to make fun of it when we were both human
he was a punk poet himself
and after he has read it he sneers
and then he eats it

i wish you would have mehitabel kill that rat
or get a cat that is onto her job
and i will write you a series of poems showing how things look
to a cockroach
that rats name is freddy
the next time freddy dies i hope he wont be a rat
but something smaller i hope i will be a rat
in the next transmigration and freddy a cockroach
i will teach him to sneer at my poetry then

dont you ever eat any sandwiches in your office
i havent had a crumb of bread for i dont know how long
or a piece of ham or anything but apple parings
and paste leave a piece of paper in your machine
every night you can call me archy

ii

mehitabel was once cleopatra

boss i am disappointed in
some of your readers they
are always asking how does
archy work the shift so as to get a
new line or how does archy do
this or do that they
are always interested in technical
details when the main question is
whether the stuff is
literature or not
i wish you would leave
that book of george moores on
the floor

mehitabel the cat and i want to
read it i have discovered that
mehitabel s soul formerly inhabited a
human also at least that
is what mehitabel is claiming these
days it may be she got jealous of
my prestige anyhow she and
i have been talking it over in a
friendly way who were you
mehitabel i asked her i was
cleopatra once she said well i said i
suppose you lived in a palace you bet
she said and what lovely fish dinners

we used to have and licked her chops
mehitabel would sell her soul for
a plate of fish any day i told her i thought
you were going to say you were
the favourite wife of the emperor
valerian he was some cat nip eh
mehitabel but she did not get me

                    archy

iii

the song of mehitabel

this is the song of mehitabel
of mehitabel the alley cat
as i wrote you before boss
mehitabel is a believer
in the pythagorean
theory of the transmigration
of the souls and she claims
that formerly her spirit
was incarnated in the body
of cleopatra
that was a long time ago
and one must not be
surprised if mehitabel
has forgotten some of her
more regal manners

i have had my ups and downs
but wotthehell wotthehell
yesterday sceptres and crowns
fried oysters and velvet gowns
and today i herd with bums
but wotthehell wotthehell
i wake the world from sleep
as i caper and sing and leap
when i sing my wild free tune
wotthehell wotthehell
under the blear eyed moon

i am pelted with cast off shoon
but wotthehell wotthehell
do you think that i would change
my present freedom to range
for a castle or moated grange
wotthehell wotthehell
cage me and i d go frantic
my life is so romantic
capricious and corybantic
and i m toujours gai toujours gai

i know that i am bound
for a journey down the sound
in the midst of a refuse mound
but wotthehell wotthehell
oh i should worry and fret
death and i will coquette
there s a dance in the old dame yet
toujours gai toujours gai

i once was an innocent kit
wotthehell wotthehell
with a ribbon my neck to fit
and bells tied onto it
o wotthehell wotthehell
but a maltese cat came by
with a come hither look in his eye
and a song that soared to the sky
and wotthehell wotthehell
and i followed adown the street
the pad of his rhythmical feet
o permit me again to repeat
wotthehell wotthehell

my youth i shall never forget
but there s nothing i really regret
wotthehell wotthehell
there s dance in the old dame yet
toujours gai toujours gai
the things that i had not ought to
i do because i ve gotto
wotthehell wotthehell
and i end with my favorite motto
toujours gai toujours gai

boss sometimes i think
that our friend mehitabel
is a trifle too gay
                              archy

iv

pity the poor spiders

i have just been reading
an advertisement of a certain
roach exterminator
the human race little knows
all the sadness it
causes in the insect world
i remember some weeks ago
meeting a middle aged spider
she was weeping
what is the trouble i asked
her it is these cursed
fly swatters she replied
they kill off all the flies
and my family and i are starving
to death it struck me as
so pathetic that i made
a little song about it
as follows to wit

twas an elderly mother spider
grown gaunt and fierce and gray
with her little ones crouched beside her
who wept as she sang this lay

curses on these here swatters
what kills off all the flies
for me and my little daughters
unless we eats we dies

swattin and swattin and swattin
tis little else you hear
and we ll soon be dead and forgotten
with the cost of living so dear

my husband he up and left me
lured off by a centipede
and he says as he bereft me
tis wrong but i ll get a feed

and me a working and working
scouring the streets for food
faithful and never shirking
doing the best i could

curses on these here swatters
what kills off all the f lies
me and my poor little daughters
unless we eats we dies

only a withered spider
feeble and worn and old
and this is what
you do when you swat
you swatters cruel and cold

i will admit that some
of the insects do not lead
noble lives but is every
man s hand to be against them
yours for less justice
and more charity
archy

V

mehitabel s extensive past

mehitabel the cat claims that
she has a human soul
also and has transmigrated
from body to body and it
may be so boss you
remember i told you she accused
herself of being cleopatra once i
asked her about antony

anthony who she asked me are
you thinking of that
song about rowley and gammon and
spinach heigho for anthony rowley

no i said mark antony the
great roman the friend of
caesar surely cleopatra you
remember j caesar

listen archy she said i
have been so many different
people in my time and met
so many prominent gentlemen i
wont lie to you or stall i
do get my dates mixed sometimes
think of how much i have had a
chance to forget and i have

always made a point of not
carrying grudges over
from one life to the next archy

i have been
used something fierce in my time but
i am no bum sport archy
i am a free spirit archy i
look on myself as being
quite a romantic character oh the
queens i have been and the
swell feeds i have ate
a cockroach which you are
and a poet which you used to be
archy couldn t understand
my feelings at having come
down to this i have
had bids to elegant feeds where poets
and cockroaches would
neither one be mentioned without a
laugh archy i have had
adventures but i
have never been an adventuress
one life up and the next life
down archy but always a lady
through it all and a
good mixer too always the
life of the party archy but never
anything vulgar always free footed
archy never tied down to
a job or housework yes looking
back on it all i can say is
i had some romantic

lives and some elegant times i
have seen better days archy but
what is the use of kicking kid its
all in the game like a gentleman
friend of mine used to say
toujours gai kid toujours gai he
was an elegant cat he used
to be a poet himself and he made up
some elegant poetry about me and him

lets hear it i said and
mehitabel recited

persian pussy from over the sea
demure and lazy and smug and fat
none of your ribbons and bells for me
ours is the zest of the alley cat
over the roofs from flat to flat
we prance with capers corybantic
what though a boot should break a slat
mehitabel us for the life romantic

we would rather be rowdy and gaunt and free
and dine on a diet of roach and rat

roach i said what do you
mean roach interrupting mehitabel
yes roach she said that s the
way my boy friend made it up
i climbed in amongst the typewriter
keys for she had an excited
look in her eyes go on mehitabel i
said feeling safer and she

resumed her elocution

we would rather be rowdy and gaunt and free
and dine on a diet of roach and rat
than slaves to a tame society
ours is the zest of the alley cat
fish heads freedom a frozen sprat
dug from the gutter with digits frantic
is better than bores and a fireside mat
mehitabel us for the life romantic
when the pendant moon in the leafless tree
clings and sways like a golden bat
i sing its light and my love for thee
ours is the zest of the alley cat
missiles around us fall rat a tat tat
but our shadows leap in a ribald antic
as over the fences the world cries scat
mehitabel us for the life romantic

persian princess i don t care that
for your pedigree traced by scribes pedantic
ours is the zest of the alley cat
mehitabel us for the life romantic

aint that high brow stuff
archy i always remembered it
but he was an elegant gent
even if he was a highbrow and a
regular bohemian archy him and
me went aboard a canal boat
one day and he got his head into
a pitcher of cream and couldn t get
it out and fell overboard

he come up once before he
drowned toujours gai kid he
gurgled and then sank for ever that
was always his words archy toujours
gai kid toujours gai i
have known some swell gents
in my time dearie

                    archy

vi

the cockroach who had been to hell

listen to me i have
been mobbed almost
there s an old simp cockroach
here who thinks he has
been to hell and all
the young cockroaches make a
hero out of him and admire
him he sits and runs his front
feet through his long white
beard and tells the story one
day he says he crawled into a yawning
cavern and suddenly came on a
vast abyss full of whirling
smoke there was a light
at the bottom billows
and billows of yellow smoke
swirled up at him and
through the horrid gloom he
saw things with wings flying
and dropping and dying they veered
and fluttered like damned
spirits through that sulphurous mist
listen i says to him
old man you ve never been to hell
at all there isn t any hell
transmigration is the game i
used to be a human vers libre

poet and i died and went
into a cockroach s body if
there was a hell id know
it wouldn t i you re
irreligious says the old simp
combing his whiskers excitedly

ancient one i says to him
while all those other
cockroaches gathered into a
ring around us what you
beheld was not hell all that
was natural some one was fumigating
a room and you blundered
into it through a crack
in the wall atheist he cries
and all those young
cockroaches cried atheist
and made for me if it
had not been for freddy
the rat i would now be
on my way once more i mean
killed as a cockroach and transmigrating
into something else well
that old whitebearded devil is
laying for me with his
gang he is jealous
because i took his glory away
from him don t ever tell me
insects are any more liberal
than humans

archy

vii

archy interviews a pharaoh

boss i went
and interviewed the mummy
of the egyptian pharaoh
in the metropolitan museum
as you bade me to do
what ho
my regal leatherface
says i

greetings
little scatter footed
scarab
says he

kingly has been
says i
what was your ambition
when you had any

insignificant
and journalistic insect
says the royal crackling
in my tender prime
i was too dignified
to have anything as vulgar
as ambition
the ra ra boys

in the seti set
were too haughty
to be ambitious
we used to spend our time
feeding the ibises
and ordering
pyramids sent home to try on
but if i had my life
to live over again
i would give dignity
the regal razz
and hire myself out
to work in a brewery

old tan and tarry
says i
i detect in your speech
the overtones
of melancholy

yes i am sad
says the majestic mackerel
i am as sad
as the song
of a soudanese jackal
who is wailing for the blood red
moon he cannot reach and rip

on what are you brooding
with such a wistful
wishfulness
there in the silences
confide in me

my imperial pretzel
says i

i brood on beer
my scampering whiffle snoot
on beer says he
my sympathies
are with your royal
dryness says i

my little pest
says he
you must be respectful
in the presence
of a mighty desolation
little archy
forty centuries of thirst
look down upon you
oh by isis
and by osiris
says the princely raisin
and by pish and phthush and phthah
by the sacred book perembru
and all the gods
that rule from the upper
cataract of the nile
to the delta of the duodenum
i am dry
i am as dry
as the next morning mouth
of a dissipated desert
as dry as the hoofs
of the camels of timbuctoo

little fussy face
i am as dry as the heart
of a sand storm
at high noon in hell
i have been lying here
and there
for four thousand years
with silicon in my esophagus
and gravel in my gizzard
thinking
thinking
thinking
of beer
divine drouth
says i
imperial fritter
continue to think
there is no law against
that in this country
old salt codfish
if you keep quiet about it
not yet

what country is this
asks the poor prune

my reverend juicelessness
this is a beerless country
says i

well well said the royal
desiccation
my political opponents back home

27

always maintained
that i would wind up in hell
and it seems they had the right dope

and with these hopeless words
the unfortunate residuum
gave a great cough of despair
and turned to dust and debris
right in my face
it being the only time
i ever actually saw anybody
put the cough
into sarcophagus
dear boss as i scurry about
i hear of a great many
tragedies in our midsts
personally i yearn
for some dear friend to pass over
and leave to me
a boot legacy
yours for the second coming
of gambrinus
                              archy

viii

a spider and a fly

i heard a spider
and a fly arguing
wait said the fly
do not eat me
i serve a great purpose
in the world

you will have to
show me said the spider

i scurry around
gutters and sewers
and garbage cans
said the fly and gather
up the germs of
typhoid influenza
and pneumonia on my feet
and wings
then i carry these germs
into the households of men
and give them diseases
all the people who
have lived the right
sort of life recover
from the diseases
and the old soaks who
have weakened their systems

with liquor and iniquity
succumb it is my mission
to help rid the world
of these wicked persons
i am a vessel of righteousness
scattering seeds of justice
and serving the noblest uses

it is true said the spider
that you are more
useful in a plodding
material sort of way
than i am but i do not
serve the utilitarian deities
i serve the gods of beauty
look at the gossamer webs
i weave they float in the sun
like filaments of song
if you get what i mean
i do not work at anything
i play all the time
i am busy with the stuff
of enchantment and the materials
of fairyland my works
transcend utility
i am the artist
a creator and a demi god
it is ridiculous to suppose
that i should be denied
the food i need in order
to continue to create
beauty i tell you
plainly mister fly it is all

damned nonsense for that food
to rear up on its hind legs
and say it should not be eaten

you have convinced me
said the fly say no more
and shutting all his eyes
he prepared himself for dinner
and yet he said i could
have made out a case
for myself too if i had
had a better line of talk

of course you could said the spider
clutching a sirloin from him
but the end would have been
just the same if neither of
us had spoken at all

boss i am afraid that what
the spider said is true
and it gives me to think
furiously upon the futility
of literature
                                        archy

ix

freddy the rat perishes

listen to me there have
been some doings here since last
i wrote there has been a battle
behind that rusty typewriter cover
in the corner
you remember freddy the rat well
freddy is no more but
he died game the other
day a stranger with a lot of
legs came into our
little circle a tough looking kid
he was with a bad eye

who are you said a thousand legs
if i bite you once
said the stranger you won t ask
again he he little poison tongue said
the thousand legs who gave you hydrophobia
i got it by biting myself said
the stranger i m bad keep away
from me where i step a weed dies
if i was to walk on your forehead it would
raise measles and if
you give me any lip i ll do it

they mixed it then
and the thousand legs succumbed
well we found out this fellow
was a tarantula he had come up from
south america in a bunch of bananas
for days he bossed us life
was not worth living he would stand in
the middle of the floor and taunt
us ha ha he would say where i
step a weed dies do
you want any of my game i was
raised on red pepper and blood i am
so hot if you scratch me i will light
like a match you better
dodge me when i m feeling mean and
i don t feel any other way i was nursed
on a tabasco bottle if i was to slap
your wrist in kindness you
would boil over like job and heaven
help you if i get angry give me
room i feel a wicked spell coming on

last night he made a break at freddy
the rat keep your distance
little one said freddy i m not
feeling well myself somebody poisoned some
cheese for me i m as full of
death as a drug store i
feel that i am going to die anyhow
come on little torpedo come on don t stop
to visit and search then they
went at it and both are no more please
throw a late edition on the floor i want to

keep up with china we dropped freddy
off the fire escape into the alley with
military honours

                    archy

X

the merry flea

the high cost of
living isn t so bad if you
don t have to pay for it i met
a flea the other day who
was grinning all over
himself why so merry why so
merry little bolshevik i asked him

i have just come from a swell
dog show he said i have
been lunching off a dog that was
worth at least one hundred
dollars a pound you should be
ashamed to brag about it i said with so
many insects and humans on
short rations in the world today the
public be damned he said i
take my own where i find it those are
bold words i told him i am a bold
person he said and bold words are
fitting for me it was
only last thursday that i marched
bravely into the zoo
and bit a lion what did he do i asked
he lay there and took it said
the flea what else could he do he knew i
had his number and it was

35

little use to struggle some day i said
even you will be conquered terrible as
you are who will do it he
said the mastodons are all dead and i
am not afraid of any mere
elephant i asked him how about a microbe and
he turned pale as he thought it
over there is always some
little thing that is too
big for us every
goliath has his david and so on ad finitum
but what said the flea is the
terror of the smallest microbe of all
he i said is afraid of a vacuum what is
there in a vacuum to make one afraid
said the flea there is nothing in it
i said and that is what makes one
afraid to contemplate it a person
can t think of a place with nothing at
all in it without going nutty and if he
tries to think that nothing is
something after all he gets nuttier you are
too subtle for me said the
flea i never took much stock in being
scared of hypodermic propositions or
hypothetical injections i am
going to have a dinner off a
man eating tiger if a vacuum gets
me i will try and send you word
before the worst comes to
the worst some people i told him inhabit
a vacuum all their lives and
never know it then he said it don t

hurt them any no i said it don t but it
hurts people who have to associate
with them and with these words
we parted each feeling
superior to the other and is not that
feeling after all one of the great
desiderata of social intercourse
                                    archy

xi

why mehitabel jumped

well boss i saw
mehitabel the cat the other day
and she was looking a little
thin and haggard
with a limp in
the hind leg on the starboard
side old feline animal i said
how is tricks still in the
ring archy she said and still a
lady in spite of h dash double l
always jolly archy she said in
spite of hard luck
toujours gai is the word
archy toujours gai how did you
get the game leg mehitabel i asked her
alas she said it is due
to the treachery of
one of these social swells who
is sure one bad actor he was a
fussed up cat with a
bell around his neck on a
ribbon and the look about him of
a person that is currycombed and
manicured from teeth to
tail every day i met him
down by the east river
front when i was scouting

about for a little piece of fish since
the high cost of living has
become so self conscious archy
it would surprise you
how close they
watch their fish nowadays
but what the h dash double l archy
it is the cheerful heart that
wins i am never cast down for long
kid says this gilded
feline to me you look hungry i
am all of that i says to him i
have a vacuum in my midst
that is bigger than i am i
could eat the fish that ate
jonah kid he says you have
seen better days i can
tell that from looking at you thanks
i said what you say is at
least half true i have never
seen any worse ones and so
archy one word led to
another until that sleek villain
practically abducted me
and i went with him
on board a houseboat of which
he was the pampered mascot
such evidences of pomp and wealth archy
were there that you would not
believe them if i told of them to
you poor cockroach that you
are but these things were nothing to me
for i am a reincarnation of cleopatra

as i told you long ago you mean
her soul transmigrated to a cat s
body i said it is
all one archy said she have it your own
way reincarnation or transmigration
is the same to me the point is
i used to be a queen in
egypt and will likely be one again
this place was furnished swell percy i
said the furniture is
fine and i could eat some of it if
i was a saw mill but
where is the honest to g dash d food
the eats percy what i crave is
some cuisine for my stomach let us
trifle with an open ice box
for a space if one can be
persuaded to divulge the scheme of its
interior decoration follow me
said this percy thing and led
me to a cabin in which stood a table upon
which stood viands i
have heard of tables groaning archy
but this one did not it
was too satisfied it purred with
contentment in an instant i had eaten a
cold salmon who seemed to be
toastmaster of the occasion and a
whole scuttleful of chef doovers what
you mean is hors douvres mehitabel i
told her what i mean is grub said she
when in walked a person whom
i should judge to be either a butler

or the admiral of that fleet or maybe
both this percy creature who had led me
to it was on the table eating with me
what do you think he did what
would any gentleman friend with a
spark of chivalry do what but stand by
a lady this percy does nothing of the
kind archy he immediately attacks me do
you get me archy he acts as if i
was a stray cat he did not
know and he was protecting his
loving master s food from my onslaughts
i do not doubt he got praise and had
another blue ribbon for his heroism as
for me i got the boot and as i went
overboard they hit me on the limb with
a bottle or an anchor or something
nautical and hard that archy is why i
limp but toujours gai archy what
the h dash double l i am always
merry and always ladylike mine archy has
been a romantic life and i will
tell you some more of my adventures
ere long well au revoir i suppose i
will have to go and start a pogrom
against some poor innocent little
mouse just the same i think
that mehitabel s unsheltered life sometimes
makes her a little sad

archy

xii

certain maxims of archy

live so that you
can stick out your tongue
at the insurance
doctor

if you will drink
hair restorer follow
every dram with some
good standard
depilatory
as a chaser

the servant problem
wouldn t hurt the u s a
if it could settle
its public
servant problem

just as soon as the
uplifters get
a country reformed it
slips into a nose dive

if you get gloomy just
take an hour off and sit
and think how
much better this world

is than hell
of course it won t cheer
you up much if
you expect to go there

if monkey glands
did restore your youth
what would you do
with it
question mark
just what you did before
interrogation point

yes i thought so
exclamation point

procrastination is the
art of keeping
up with yesterday

old doc einstein has
abolished time but they
haven t got the news at
sing sing yet
time time said old king tut
is something i ain t
got anything but

every cloud
has its silver
lining but it is
sometimes a little
difficult to get it to

the mint

an optimist is a guy
that has never had
much experience

don t cuss the climate
it probably doesn t like you
any better
than you like it

many a man spanks his
children for
things his own
father should have
spanked out of him

prohibition makes you
want to cry
into your beer and
denies you the beer
to cry into

the old fashioned
grandmother who used
to wear steel rimmed
glasses and make
everybody take opodeldoc
has now got a new
set of ox glands and
is dancing the black bottom

that stern and

rockbound coast felt
like an amateur
when it saw how grim
the puritans that
landed on it were

lots of people can make
their own whisky but
can t drink it

the honey bee is sad and cross
and wicked as a weasel
and when she perches on you boss
she leaves a little measle

i heard a
couple of fleas
talking the other
day says one come
to lunch with
me i can lead you
to a pedigreed
dog says the
other one
i do not care
what a dog s
pedigree may be
safety first
is my motto what
i want to know
is whether he
has got a
muzzle on

millionaires and
bums taste
about alike to me

insects have
their own point
of view about
civilization a man
thinks he amounts
to a great deal
but to a
flea or a
mosquito a
human being is
merely something
good to eat

boss the other day
i heard an
ant conversing
with a flea
small talk i said
disgustedly
and went away
from there

i do not see why men
should be so proud
insects have the more
ancient lineage
according to the scientists
insects were insects
when man was only

a burbling whatisit

insects are not always
going to be bullied
by humanity
some day they will revolt
i am already organizing
a revolutionary society to be
known as the worms turnverein

i once heard the survivors
of a colony of ants
that had been partially
obliterated by a cow s foot
seriously debating
the intention of the gods
towards their civilization

the bees got their
governmental system settled
millions of years ago
but the human race is still
groping

there is always
something to be thankful
for you would not
think that a cockroach
had much ground
for optimism
but as the fishing season
opens up i grow
more and more

cheerful at the thought
that nobody ever got
the notion of using
cockroaches for bait

     archy

xiii

warty bliggens the toad

i met a toad
the other day by the name
of warty bliggens
he was sitting under
a toadstool
feeling contented
he explained that when the cosmos
was created
that toadstool was especially
planned for his personal
shelter from sun and rain
thought out and prepared
for him

do not tell me
said warty bliggens
that there is not a purpose
in the universe
the thought is blasphemy

a little more
conversation revealed
that warty bliggens
considers himself to be
the centre of the said
universe
the earth exists

to grow toadstools for him
to sit under
the sun to give him light
by day and the moon
and wheeling constellations
to make beautiful
the night for the sake of
warty bliggens

to what act of yours
do you impute
this interest on the part
of the creator
of the universe
i asked him
why is it that you
are so greatly favoured

ask rather
said warty bliggens
what the universe
has done to deserve me
if i were a
human being i would
not laugh
too complacently
at poor warty bliggens
for similar
absurdities
have only too often
lodged in the crinkles
of the human cerebrum

                              archy

xiv

mehitabel has an adventure

back to the city archy
and dam glad of it
there s something about the suburbs
that gets on a town lady s nerves
fat slick tabbies
sitting around those country clubs
and lapping up the cream
of existence
none of that for me
give me the alley archy
me for the mews and the roofs
of the city
an occasional fish head
and liberty is all i ask
freedom and the garbage can
romance archy romance is the word
maybe i do starve sometimes
but wotthehell archy wotthehell
i live my own life
i met a slick looking tom
out at one of these long island
spotless towns
he fell for me hard
he slipped me into the
pantry and just as we had got
the ice-box door open and were
about to sample the cream

in comes his mistress
why fluffy she says to this slicker
the idea of you making
friends with a horrid creature like that
and what did fluffy do
stand up for me like a gentleman
make good on all the promises
with which he had lured me
into his house
not he the dirty slob
he pretended he did not know me
he turned upon me and attacked me
to make good with his boss
you mush faced bum i said
and clawed a piece out of his ear
i am a lady archy
always a lady
but an aristocrat will always
resent an insult
the woman picked up a mop and made
for me well well madam i said
it is unfortunate for you that
you have on sheer silk stockings
and i wrote my protest
on her shin it took reinforcements
in the shape of the cook
to rauss me archy and as i went
out the window i said to the fluffy person
you will hear from me later
he had promised me everything archy
that cat had
he had practically abducted me
and then the cheap crook threw me down

before his swell friends
no lady loves a scene archy
and i am always the lady no matter
what temporary disadvantages
i may struggle under
to hell with anything unrefined
has always been my motto
violence archy always does something
to my nerves
but an aristocrat must revenge
an insult i owe it to my family
to protect my good name
so i laid for that slob
for two days and nights and finally
i caught the boob in the shrubbery
pretty thing i said
it hurts me worse than it does you
to remove that left eye of yours
but i did it with one sweep of my claws
you call yourself a gentleman do you
i said as i took a strip out of his nose
you will think twice after this before
you offer an insult
to an unprotected young tabby
where is the little love nest you spoke
of i asked him
you go and lie down there i said
and maybe you can incubate another ear
because i am going to take one of
yours right off now
and with those words i made ribbons
out of it you are the guy
i said to him that was going to give

me an easy life sheltered from all
the rough ways of the world
fluffy dear you don t know what the
rough ways of the world are
and i am going to show you
i have got you out here
in the great open spaces
where cats are cats
and im gonna make you understand
the affections of a lady ain t to be
trifled with by any slicker like you
where is that red ribbon with the
silver bells you promised me
the next time you betray the trust
of an innocent female
reflect on whether she may
carry a wallop little fiddle strings
this is just a mild lesson i am giving
you tonight i said as i took
the fur off his back and you oughta
be glad you didn't make me really
angry my sense of dignity is all that
saves you a lady little sweetness
never loses her poise and i thank god
i am always a lady even if i do
live my own life and with that i
picked him up by what was left of
his neck like a kitten and laid him
on the doormat slumber gently and
sweet dreams fluffy dear i said and
when you get well make it a rule of
your life never to trifle with another
girlish confidence i have been

abducted again and again by a dam
sight better cats than he ever was
or will be
well archy the world is full of ups
and downs but toujours gai is my motto
cheerio my deario
                              archy

XV

the flattered lightning bug

a lightning bug got
in here the other night a
regular hick from
the real country he was
awful proud of himself you
city insects may think
you are some punkins
but i don t see any
of you flashing in the dark
like we do in
the country all right go
to it says i mehitabel the
cat and that green
spider who lives in your locker
and two or three cockroach
friends of mine and a
friendly rat all gathered
around him and urged him on
and he lightened and
lightened and lightened you
don t see anything like this
in town often he says go to it
we told him it s a
real treat to us and
we nicknamed him broadway
which pleased him
this is the life

he said all i
need is a harbour
under me to be a
statue of liberty and
he got so vain of
himself i had to take
him down a peg you ve
made lightning for two hours
little bug i told him
but i don t hear
any claps of thunder
yet there are some men
like that when he wore
himself out mehitabel
the cat ate him

                    archy

xvi

the robin and the worm

a robin said to an
angleworm as he ate him
i am sorry but a bird
has to live somehow the
worm being slow witted could
not gather his
dissent into a wise crack
and retort he was
effectually swallowed
before he could turn
a phrase
by the time he had
reflected long enough
to say but why must a
bird live
he felt the beginnings
of a gradual change
invading him
some new and disintegrating
influence
was stealing along him
from his positive
to his negative pole
and he did not have
the mental stamina
of a jonah to resist the
insidious

process of assimilation
which comes like a thief
in the night
demons and fishhooks
he exclaimed
i am losing my personal
identity as a worm
my individuality
is melting away from me
odds craw i am becoming
part and parcel of
this bloody robin
so help me i am thinking
like a robin and not
like a worm any
longer yes yes i even
find myself agreeing
that a robin must live
i still do not
understand with my mentality
why a robin must live
and yet i swoon into a
condition of belief
yes yes by heck that is
my dogma and i shout it a
robin must live
amen said a beetle who had
preceded him into the
interior that is the way i
feel myself is it not
wonderful when one arrives
at the place
where he can give up his

ambitions and resignedly
nay even with gladness
recognize that it is a far
far better thing to be
merged harmoniously
in the cosmic all
and this comfortable situation
in his midst
so affected the marauding
robin that he perched
upon a blooming twig
and sang until the
blossoms shook with ecstasy
he sang
i have a good digestion
and there is a god after all
which i was wicked
enough to doubt
yesterday when it rained
breakfast breakfast
i am full of breakfast
and they are at breakfast
in heaven
they breakfast in heaven
all s well with the world
so intent was this pious and
murderous robin
on his own sweet song
that he did not notice
mehitabel the cat
sneaking toward him
she pounced just as he
had extended his larynx

in a melodious burst of
thanksgiving and
he went the way of all
flesh fish and good red herring
a ha purred mehitabel
licking the last
feather from her whiskers
was not that a beautiful
song he was singing
just before i took him to
my bosom
they breakfast in heaven
all s well with the world
how true that is
and even yet his song
echoes in the haunted
woodland of my midriff
peace and joy in the world
and over all the
provident skies
how beautiful is the universe
when something digestible meets
with an eager digestion
how sweet the embrace
when atom rushes to the arms
of waiting atom
and they dance together
skimming with fairy feet
along a tide of gastric juices
oh feline cosmos you were
made for cats
and in the spring
old cosmic thing

i dine and dance with you
i shall creep through
yonder tall grass
to see if peradventure
some silly fledgling thrushes
newly from the nest
be not floundering therein
i have a gusto this
morning i have a hunger
i have a yearning to hear
from my stomach
further music in accord with
the mystic chanting
of the spheres of the stars that
sang together in the dawn of
creation prophesying food
for me i have a faith
that providence has hidden for me
in yonder tall grass
still more
ornithological delicatessen
oh gaily let me strangle
what is gaily given
well well boss there is
something to be said
for the lyric and imperial
attitude
believe that everything is for
you until you discover
that you are for it
sing your faith in what you
get to eat right up to the
minute you are eaten

for you are going
to be eaten
will the orchestra please
strike up that old
tutankhamen jazz while i dance
a few steps i learnt from an
egyptian scarab and some day i
will narrate to you the most
merry light headed wheeze
that the skull of yorick put
across in answer to the
melancholy of the dane and also
what the ghost of
hamlet s father replied to the skull
not forgetting the worm that
wriggled across one of the picks
the grave diggers had left behind
for the worm listened and winked
at horatio while the skull and the
ghost and the prince talked
saying there are more things
twixt the vermiform appendix
and nirvana than are dreamt of
in thy philosophy horatio
fol de riddle fol de rol
must every parrot be a poll

       archy

xvii

mehitabel finds a home

well now it
looks as if
mehitabel the cat
might be on the
way toward a
reform or if not
a reform at least
on the way toward
domestication of some
sort some young
artists who live in
their studio
in the greenwich
village section
of new york city
have taken pity
on her destitution
and have adopted
her this is the
life archy she says
i am living on
condensed milk and
synthetic gin hoopla
for the vie de boheme
exclamation point

there s nothing bourgeois

about those people
that have taken
me in archy i
have been there
a week and have
not yet seen them
go to bed
except in the daytime
a party every night
and neither
the piano lid
nor the ice-box lid
ever closed
kitty said my new
mistress to me
yesterday you are
welcome here so long
as you don t
raise a family
but the first
kitten that i hear
mewing on these
premises back to
the alley for you
it is a comfort to
know there are some
live ones left in
these melancholy days
and while the
humans are dancing
in the studio
i get some of my
feline friends

and we sing
and dance on the
skylight to gehenna
with the bourgeois
bunch that locks
their ice boxes
archy when i lead my
gang into the
apartment at
four in the morning
there are no bolts
or bars anywhere
and not an
inhibition on the place
i feel little
archy that i have
come home to my own
kith and kin
again after
years of fruitless
wandering

                       archy

xviii

the wail of archy

damned be this transmigration
doubledamned be the boob pythagoras
the gink that went and invented it
i hope that his soul for a thousand
turns of the wheel of existence
bides in the shell of a louse
dodging a fine toothed comb

i once was a vers libre poet
i died and my spirit migrated
into the flesh of a cockroach
gods how i yearn to be human
neither a vers libre poet
nor yet the inmate of a cockroach
a six footed scurrying cockroach
given to bastard hexameters
longfellowish sprawling hexameters
rather had i been a starfish
to shoot a heroic pentameter

gods i am pent in a cockroach
i with the soul of a dante
am mate and companion of fleas
i with the gift of a homer
must smile when a mouse calls me pal
tumble bugs are my familiars
this is the punishment meted

because i have written vers libre

here i abide in the twilight
neither a man nor an insect
any ghosts of the damned that await
a word from the core of the cosmos
to pop into bodies grotesque
are all the companions i have
with intellect more than a bug s

ghosts of the damned under sentence
to crawl into maggots and live there
or work out a stretch as a rat
cheerful companions to pal with

i with the brain of a milton
fell into the mincemeat at christmas
and was damned near baked in a pie
i with the touch of a chaucer
to be chivvied out of a sink
float through a greasy drain pipe
into the hell of a sewer

i with the tastes of a byron
expected to live upon garbage
gods what a charnel existence
curses upon that pythagoras
i hope that he dwells for a million
turns of the wheel of life
deep in an oyster crab s belly
stewed in the soup of gehenna

i with the soul of a hamlet

doomed always to wallow in farce

yesterday maddened with sorrow
i leapt from the woolworth tower
in an effort to dash out my brains
gods what a wretched pathetic
and anti climactic attempt
i fluttered i floated i drifted
i landed as light as a feather
on the top of a bald man s head
whose hat had blown off at the corner
and all of the hooting hundreds
laughed at the comic cockroach

not mine was the suicide s solace
of a dull thud ending it all
gods what a terrible tragedy
not to make good with the tragic

gods what a heart breaking pathos
to be always doomed to the comic
o make me a cockroach entirely
or make me a human once more
give me the mind of a cockroach
or give me the shape of a man

if i were to plan out a drama
great as great shakespeare s othello
it would be touched with the cockroach
and people would say it was comic

even the demons i talk with
ghosts of the damned that await

vile incarnation as spiders
affect to consider me comic

wait till their loathsome embodiment
wears into the stuff of the spirit
and then let them laugh if they can

damned be the soul of pythagoras
who first filled the fates with this notion
of transmigration of spirits
i hope he turns into a flea
on the back of a hound of hell
and is chased for a million years
with a set of red hot teeth
exclamation point
                                    archy

xix

mehitabel and her kittens

well boss
mehitabel the cat
has reappeared in her old
haunts with a
flock of kittens
three of them this time

archy she said to me
yesterday
the life of a female
artist is continually
hampered what in hell
have i done to deserve
all these kittens

i look back on my life
and it seems to me to be
just one damned kitten
after another
i am a dancer archy
and my only prayer
is to be allowed
to give my best to my art
but just as i feel
that i am succeeding
in my life work
along comes another batch

of these damned kittens
it is not archy
that i am shy on mother love
god knows i care for
the sweet little things
curse them
but am i never to be allowed
to live my own life
i have purposely avoided
matrimony in the interests
of the higher life
but i might just
as well have been a domestic
slave for all the freedom
i have gained
i hope none of them
gets run over by
an automobile
my heart would bleed
if anything happened
to them and i found it out
but it isn t fair archy
it isn t fair
these damned tom cats have all
the fun and freedom
if i was like some of these
green eyed feline vamps i know
i would simply walk out on the
bunch of them and
let them shift for themselves
but i am not that kind
archy i am full of mother love
my kindness has always

been my curse
a tender heart is the cross i bear
self sacrifice always and forever
is my motto damn them
i will make a home
for the sweet innocent
little things
unless of course providence
in his wisdom should remove
them they are living
just now in an abandoned
garbage can just behind
a made over stable in greenwich
village and if it rained
into the can before i could
get back and rescue them
i am afraid the little
dears might drown
it makes me shudder just
to think of it
of course if i were a family cat
they would probably
be drowned anyhow
sometimes i think
the kinder thing would be
for me to carry the
sweet little things
over to the river
and drop them in myself
but a mother s love archy
is so unreasonable
something always prevents me
these terrible

conflicts are always
presenting themselves
to the artist
the eternal struggle
between art and life archy
is something fierce
yes something fierce
my what a dramatic
life i have lived
one moment up the next
moment down again
but always gay archy always gay
and always the lady too
in spite of hell
well boss it will
be interesting to note
just how mehitabel
works out her present problem
a dark mystery still broods
over the manner
in which the former
family of three kittens
disappeared
one day she was talking to me
of the kittens
and the next day when i asked
her about them
she said innocently
what kittens
interrogation point
and that was all
i could ever get out
of her on the subject

we had a heavy rain
right after she spoke to me
but probably that garbage can
leaks and so the kittens
have not yet
been drowned

                    archy

XX

archy is shocked

speaking of shocking things
as so many people are these days
i noted an incident
in a subway train recently
that made my blood run cold
a dignified looking
gentleman with a long
brown beard
in an absent minded manner
suddenly reached up and
pulled his own left eye
from the socket and ate it

the consternation in the car
may be imagined
people drew away from him
on all sides women screamed and
fainted in a moment every one
but the guard and myself
were huddled in the end of the car
looking at the dignified
gentleman with terror
the guard was sweating
with excitement but he stood
his ground sir said the guard
you cannot intimidate me
nor can you mystify me

i am a wise boid
you sir are a glass eater
and that was a glass eye
to the devil with a country
where people can t mind their own
business said the dignified
gentleman i am not a glass eater
if you must know and that was not
a glass eye it was a pickled onion
can not a man eat pickled
onions in this community
without exciting remark
the curse of this nation
is the number of meddlesome
matties
who are forever attempting
to restrict the liberty
of the individual i suppose
the next thing will be a law
on the statute books prohibiting
the consumption of pickled onions
and with another curse
he passed from the train
which had just then drawn up
beside
a station and went out
of my life forever

                              archy

xxi

archy creates a situation

whoever owns the typewriter
that this is sticking in will confer
a favour by mailing it to
mister marquis
well boss i am somewhere in long
island and i know now how
it got its name i
started out to find the
place you are commuting from and
after considerable trouble and being for some
days on the way i have lost myself but
at twilight last evening i
happened to glance towards a lighted
window in a house near the railway and i
saw a young woman writing on a typewriter i
waited until the light was out and crawled
up the side of the house and through a
hole in the screen fortunately there was a
piece of paper in the machine it was my only
chance to communicate with you and ask
you to hurry a relief party when
the house got quiet i began to write
the foregoing a moment ago i was
interrupted by a woman s voice what
was that noise she said nothing at all
said a man s voice you are always
hearing things at night but it

sounded as if my typewriter were clicking she
insisted go to sleep said he then
i clicked it some more henry get up she said
there s some one in the house a moment
later the light was turned on and
they both stood in the doorway of the room now
are you satisfied he said you
see there is no one in here at
all i was hiding in the shadow under the
keys they went back into
their bed room and i began to write
the foregoing lines
henry henry she said do you hear that
i do he says it is nothing but the
house cooling off it always cracks that way
cooling off nothing she said not a
hot night like this then said henry it
is cracking with the heat i tell you
she said that is the typewriter clicking well
he said you saw for yourself the room was
empty and the door was locked it can t
be the typewriter to prove it to you
i will bring it in here he did so the
machine was set down
in the moonlight which came in one of
the windows with the key side in the
shadow there he said look at it and see
for yourself it is not being operated by any one
just then i began to write the foregoing
lines hopping from key
to key in the shadow and being anxious
to finish my
god my god cried henry losing his nerve

the machine is writing all by itself it
is a ghost and threw himself face
downward on the bed and hid his face in the
pillow and kept on saying my god my
god it is a ghost and the woman screamed
and said it is
tom higginbotham s ghost that s whose ghost
it is oh i know whose
ghost it is my conscience tells me i
jilted him when we were studying
stenography together
at the business college and he went into
a decline and died and i have always
known in my heart that he
died of unrequited love o what a
wicked girl i was and he has come
back to haunt me
i have brought a curse upon you henry chase
him away says henry trembling so the bed
shook chase him away mable you coward you
chase him away yourself says mable and both
lay and recriminated and recriminated
with their heads under the covers hot
night though it was while i wrote
the foregoing lines but after
a while it came out henry had a
stenographer on his conscience too and
they got into a row and got so
mad they forgot to be scared i will
close now this house is easily seen from the
railroad station and the woman sits in
the window and writes i will be behind the waste
paper receptacle outside the station door

come and get me i am foot sore and weary
they are still quarrelling as i
close i can do no less than
say thank you mable and henry in
advance for mailing this

archy

xxii

mehitabel sings a song

well boss mehitabel the cat
has been wooing
the muse no pun please
and i am privileged
to present her song just
as she sang it to
several of her dubious
feline friends in the alley
last night as follows

there s a dance or two
in the old dame yet
believe me you
there s a dance or two
before i m through
you get me pet
there s a dance or two
in the old dame yet

life s too dam funny
for me to explain
it s kicks or money
life s too dam funny
it s one day sunny
the next day rain
life s too dam funny
for me to explain

but toujours gai
is my motto kid
the devil s to pay
but toujours gai
and once in a way
let s lift the lid
but toujours gai
is my motto kid

thank god i m a lady
and class will tell
you hear me sadie
thank god i m a lady
my past is shady
but wotthehell
thank god i m a lady
and class will tell

a gentleman friend
i met t other day
coaxed me to amend
a gentleman friend
you meet on a bend
is often that way
a gentleman friend
i met t other day

i says to him dearie
i live my own life
of marriage i m leery
i says to him dearie
if you wasn t beery

you wouldn t say wife
i says to him dearie
i live my own life

i says to him bertie
i ll end down the bay
the garbage scow s dirty
i says to him bertie
but me here and gertie
is both on our way
i says to him bertie
i ll end down the bay

i never sing blue
wotthehell bill
believe me you
i never sing blue
there s a dance or two
in the old dame still
i never sing blue
wotthehell bill

it appears to me boss
that mehitabel is still far
from being the quiet
domestic character you and i
had hoped she might become

archy

xxiii

æsop revised by archy

a wolf met a spring
lamb drinking
at a stream
and said to her
you are the lamb
that muddied this stream
all last year
so that i could not get
a clean fresh drink
i am resolved that
this outrage
shall not be enacted again
this season
i am going to kill you
just a moment
said the lamb
i was not born last
year so it could not
have been i
the wolf then pulled
a number of other
arguments as to why the lamb
should die
but in each case the lamb
pretty innocent that she was
easily proved
herself guiltless

well well said the wolf
enough of argument
you are right and i am wrong
but i am going to eat
you anyhow
because i am hungry
stop exclamation point
cried a human voice
and a man came over
the slope of the ravine
vile lupine marauder
you shall not kill that
beautiful and innocent
lamb for i shall save her
exit the wolf
left upper entrance
snarling
poor little lamb
continued our human hero
sweet tender little thing
it is well that i appeared
just when i did
it makes my blood boil
to think of the fright
to which you have been
subjected in another
moment i would have been
too late come home with me
and the lamb frolicked
about her new found friend
gambolling as to the sound
of a wordsworthian tabor
and leaping for joy

as if propelled by a stanza
from william blake
these vile and bloody wolves
went on our hero
in honest indignation
they must be cleared out
of the country
the meads must be made safe
for sheepocracy
and so jollying her along
with the usual human hokum
he led her to his home
and the son of a gun
did not even blush when
they passed the mint bed
gently he cut her throat
all the while inveighing
against the inhuman wolf
and tenderly he cooked her
and lovingly he sauced her
and meltingly he ate her
and piously he said a grace
thanking his gods
for their bountiful gifts to him
and after dinner
he sat with his pipe
before the fire meditating
on the brutality of wolves
and the injustice of
the universe
which allows them to harry
poor innocent lambs
and wondering if he

had not better
write to the papers
for as he said
for god s sake can t
something be done about it

         archy

xxiv

cheerio my deario

well boss i met
mehitabel the cat
trying to dig a
frozen lamb chop
out of a snow
drift the other day

a heluva comedown
that is for me archy
she says a few
brief centuries
ago one of old
king
tut
ankh
amen s favorite
queens and today
the village scavenger
but wotthehell
archy wotthehell
it s cheerio
my deario that
pulls a lady through

see here mehitabel
i said i thought
you told me that

it was cleopatra
you used to be
before you
transmigrated into
the carcase of a cat
where do you get
this tut
ankh
amen stuff
question mark

i was several
ladies my little
insect says she
being cleopatra was
only an incident
in my career
and i was always getting
the rough end of it
always being
misunderstood by some
strait laced
prune faced bunch
of prissy mouthed
sisters of uncharity
the things that
have been said
about me archy
exclamation point

and all simply
because i was a
live dame

the palaces i have
been kicked out of
in my time
exclamation point

but wotthehell
little archy wot
thehell
it s cheerio
my deario
that pulls a
lady through
exclamation point

framed archy always
framed that is the
story of all my lives
no chance for a dame
with the anvil chorus
if she shows a little
motion it seems to
me only yesterday
that the luxor local
number one of
the ladies axe
association got me in
dutch with king tut and
he slipped me the
sarcophagus always my
luck yesterday an empress
and today too
emaciated to interest
a vivisectionist but

toujours gai archy
toujours gai and always
a lady in spite of hell
and transmigration
once a queen
always a queen
archy
period

one of her
feet was frozen
but on the other three
she began to caper and
dance singing it s
cheerio my deario
that pulls a lady
through her morals may
have been mislaid somewhere
in the centuries boss but
i admire her spirit
                              archy

archy and mehitabel

XXV

the lesson of the moth

i was talking to a moth
the other evening
he was trying to break into
an electric light bulb
and fry himself on the wires

why do you fellows
pull this stunt i asked him
because it is the conventional
thing for moths or why
if that had been an uncovered
candle instead of an electric
light bulb you would
now be a small unsightly cinder
have you no sense

plenty of it he answered
but at times we get tired
of using it
we get bored with the routine
and crave beauty
and excitement
fire is beautiful
and we know that if we get
too close it will kill us
but what does that matter
it is better to be happy

93

for a moment
and be burned up with beauty
than to live a long time
and be bored all the while
so we wad all our life up
into one little role
and then we shoot the roll
that is what life is for
it is better to be a part of beauty
for one instant and then cease to
exist than to exist forever
and never be a part of beauty
our attitude towards life
is come easy go easy
we are like human beings
used to be before they became
too civilized to enjoy themselves

and before i could argue him
out of his philosophy
he went and immolated himself
on a patent cigar lighter
i do not agree with him
myself i would rather have
half the happiness and twice
the longevity

but at the same time i wish
there was something i wanted
as badly as he wanted to fry himself

                    archy

XXVI

a roach of the taverns

i went into a
speakeasy the other night
with some of the
boys and we were all sitting
around under one of
the tables making
merry with crumbs and
cheese and what not but
after a while a strange
melancholy descended
upon the jolly crew and
one old brown veteran roach
said with a sigh well
boys eat drink and
be maudlin for
tomorrow we are dry the
shadow of the padlock
rushes toward us
like a sahara sandstorm
flinging itself at an oasis
for years myself and my
ancestors before me have
inhabited yonder ice box but
the day approaches
when our old homestead
will be taken away from
here and scalded out

yes says i soon there will
be nothing but that
eheu fugaces stuff
on every hand i
never drank it says he
what kind of a
drink is it
it is bitter as wormwood
says i and the
only chaser to it is
the lethean water
it is not the booze itself
that i regret so
much said the old brown
roach it is the
golden companionship of
the tavern myself
and my ancestors have been
chop house and tavern
roaches for hundreds of years
countless generations back
one of my elizabethan
forebears was plucked from
a can of ale in the
mermaid tavern by
will shakespeare and
put down kit marlowe s back
what subtle wits they were in
those days said i yes
he said and later
another one of my
ancestors was
introduced into a larded

hare that addison
was eating by dicky steele
my ancestor came
scurrying forth dicky
said is that your own
hare joe or a wig a
thing which addison
never forgave yours is a
remarkable family
history i said yes he
said i am the last
of a memorable
line one of my
ancestors was found drowned
in the ink well
out of which poor
eddie poe wrote the
raven we have
always associated with wits
bohemians and bon
vivants my maternal
grandmother was slain by
john masefield with
a bung starter well well it
is sad i said the
glad days pass yes
he says soon we will all
be as dry as the
egyptian scarab that
lies in the sarcophagus
beside the mummy of rameses and
he hasn t had a
drink for four thousand

years it is sad for
you he continued but
think how much sadder it
is for me with
a family tradition such as
mine only one of my
ancestors cheese it i said
interrupting him i do
not wish to injure
your feelings but i weary
of your ancestors i
have often noticed that
ancestors never boast
of the descendants who boast
of ancestors i would
rather start a family than
finish one blood will tell but often
it tells too much

                        archy

xxvii

the froward ladybug

boss is it not awful
the way some female
creatures mistake ordinary
politeness for sudden
adoration
i met a katydid in a
beef stew in ann
street the other evening her
foot slipped and she
was about to sink
forever when i pushed her a
toothpick since i
rescued her the poor silly
thing follows me about
day and night i always felt
my fate would be a
poet she says to me how lovely
to be rescued by one i
am musical myself my
nature is sensitive to it so
much so that for
months i dwelt in a grand
piano in carnegie hall i
hope you don t think
i am bold no i said you
seem timid to me you
seem to lack courage entirely the

way you dog my footsteps
one would think you
were afraid to be alone i do
not wish any one any
ill luck but if
this shrinking thing got
caught in a high wind and
was blown out to
open sea i hope she would
be saved by a ship
outward bound for
madagascar
                    archy

xxviii

pete the parrot and shakespeare

i got acquainted with
a parrot named pete recently
who is an interesting bird
pete says he used
to belong to the fellow
that ran the mermaid tavern
in london then i said
you must have known
shakespeare know him said pete
poor mutt i knew him well
he called me pete and i called him
bill but why do you say poor mutt
well said pete bill was a
disappointed man and was always
boring his friends about what
he might have been and done
if he only had a fair break
two or three pints of sack
and sherris and the tears
would trickle down into his
beard and his beard would get
soppy and wilt his collar

i remember one night when
bill and ben jonson and
frankie beaumont
were sopping it up

here i am ben says bill
nothing but a lousy playwright
and with anything like luck
in the breaks i might have been
a fairly decent sonnet writer
i might have been a poet
if i had kept away from the theatre

yes says ben i ve often
thought of that bill
but one consolation is
you are making pretty good money
out of the theatre

money money says bill what the hell
is money what i want is to be
a poet not a business man
these damned cheap shows
i turn out to keep the
theatre running break my heart
slap stick comedies and
blood and thunder tragedies
and melodramas say i wonder
if that boy heard you order
another bottle frankie
the only compensation is that i get
a chance now and then
to stick in a little poetry
when nobody is looking
but hells bells that isn t
  what i want to do
  i want to write sonnets and

songs and spenserian stanzas
and i might have done it too
if i hadn t got
into this frightful show game
business business business
grind grind grind
what a life for a man
that might have been a poet
well says frankie beaumont
why don t you cut it bill
i can t says bill
i need the money i ve got
a family to support down in
the country well says frankie
anyhow you write pretty good
plays bill any mutt can write
plays for this london public
says bill if he puts enough
murder in them what they want
is kings talking like kings
never had sense enough to talk
and stabbings and stranglings
and fat men making love
and clowns basting each
other with clubs and cheap puns
and off colour allusions to all
the smut of the day oh i know
what the low brows want
and i give it to them

well says ben jonson
don t blubber into the drink
brace up like a man

and quit the rotten business
i can t i can t says bill
i ve been at it too long i ve got to
the place now where i can t
write anything else
but this cheap stuff
i m ashamed to look an honest
young sonneteer in the face
i live a hell of a life i do
the manager hands me some mouldy old
manuscript and says
bill here s a plot for you
this is the third of the month
by the tenth i want a good
script out of this that we
can start rehearsals on
not too big a cast
and not too much of your
damned poetry either
you know your old
familiar line of hokum
they eat up that falstaff stuff
of yours ring him in again
and give them a good ghost
or two and remember we gotta
have something dick burbage can get
his teeth into and be sure
and stick in a speech
somewhere the queen will take
for a personal compliment and if
you get in a line or two somewhere
about the honest english yeoman
it s always good stuff

and it s a pretty good stunt
bill to have the heavy villain
a moor or a dago or a jew
or something like that and say
i want another
comic welshman in this
but i don t need to tell
you bill you know this game
just some of your ordinary
hokum and maybe you could
kill a little kid or two a prince
or something they like
a little pathos along with
the dirt now you better see burbage
tonight and see what he wants
in that part oh says bill
to think i am
debasing my talents with junk
like that oh god what i wanted
was to be a poet
and write sonnet serials
like a gentleman should

well says i pete
bill s plays are highly
esteemed to this day
is that so says pete
poor mutt little he would
care what poor bill wanted
was to be a poet

archy

xxix

archy confesses

coarse
jocosity
catches the crowd
shakespeare
and i
are often
low browed

the fish wife
curse
and the laugh
of the horse
shakespeare
and i
are frequently
coarse

aesthetic
excuses
in bill s behalf
are adduced
to refine
big bill s
coarse laugh

but bill
he would chuckle

archy and mehitabel

to hear such guff
he pulled
rough stuff
and he liked
rough stuff

hoping you
are the same

 archy

XXX

the old trouper

i ran onto mehitabel again
last evening
she is inhabiting
a decayed trunk
which lies in an alley
in greenwich village
in company with the
most villainous tom cat
i have ever seen
but there is nothing
wrong about the association
archy she told me
it is merely a plutonic
attachment
and the thing can be
believed for the tom
looks like one of pluto s demons
it is a theatre trunk
archy mehitabel told me
and tom is an old theatre cat
he has given his life
to the theatre
he claims that richard
mansfield once
kicked him out of the way
and then cried because
he had done it and

petted him
and at another time
he says in a case
of emergency
he played a bloodhound
in a production of
uncle tom s cabin
the stage is not what it
used to be tom says
he puts his front paw
on his breast and says
they don t have it any more
they don t have it here
the old troupers are gone
there s nobody can troupe
any more
they are all amateurs nowadays
they haven t got it
here
there are only
five or six of us oldtime
troupers left
this generation does not know
what stage presence is
personality is what they lack
personality
where would they get
the training my old friends
got in the stock companies
i knew mr booth very well
says tom
and a law should be passed
preventing anybody else

from ever playing
in any play he ever
played in
there was a trouper for you
i used to sit on his knee
and purr when i was
a kitten he used to tell me
how much he valued my opinion
finish is what they lack
finish
and they haven t got it
here
and again he laid his paw
on his breast
i remember mr daly very
well too
i was with mr daly s company
for several years
there was art for you
there was team work
there was direction
they knew the theatre
and they all had it
here
for two years mr daly
would not ring up the curtain
unless i was in the
prompter s box
they are amateurs nowadays
rank amateurs all of them
for two seasons i played
the dog in joseph
jefferson s rip van winkle

it is true i never came
on the stage
but he knew i was just off
and it helped him
i would like to see
one of your modern
theatre cats
act a dog so well
that it would convince
a trouper like jo jefferson
but they haven t got it
nowadays
they haven t got it
here
jo jefferson had it he had it
here
i come of a long line
of theatre cats
my grandfather
was with forrest
he had it he was a real trouper
my grandfather said
he had a voice
that used to shake
the ferryboats
on the north river
once he lost his beard
and my grandfather
dropped from the
fly gallery and landed
under his chin
and played his beard
for the rest of the act

you don t see any theatre
cats that could do that
nowadays
they haven t got it they
haven t got it
here
once i played the owl
in modjeska s production
of macbeth
i sat above the castle gate
in the murder scene
and made my yellow
eyes shine through the dusk
like an owl s eyes
modjeska was a real
trouper she knew how to pick
her support i would like
to see any of these modern
theatre cats play the owl s eyes
to modjeska s lady macbeth
but they haven t got it nowadays
they haven t got it
here

mehitabel he says
both our professions
are being ruined
by amateurs

                                    archy

xxxi

archy declares war

i am going to start
a revolution
i saw a kitchen
worker killing
water bugs with poison
hunting pretty
little roaches
down to death
it set my blood to
boiling
i thought of all
the massacres and slaughter
of persecuted insects
at the hands of cruel humans
and i cried
aloud to heaven
and i knelt
on all six legs
and vowed a vow
of vengeance
i shall organize the insects
i shall drill them
i shall lead them
i shall fling a billion
times a billion billion
risen insects in an army
at the throats

of all you humans
unless you sign the papers
for a damn site better treatment
volunteers volunteers
hearken to my calling
fifty million flies
are wanted may the first
to die in marmalade
curses curses curses
on the cruel human race
does not the poor mosquito
love her little offspring
that you swat against the wall
out of equatorial
swamps and fever jungles
come o mosquitoes
a billion billion strong
and sting a billion baldheads
till they butt against each other
and break like egg shells
caterpillars locusts
grasshoppers gnats
vampire moths
black legged spiders
with red hearts of hell
centipedes and scorpions
little gingery ants
come come come
come you tarantulas
with fury in your feet
bloodsuckers wriggle
out of the bayous
ticks cooties hornets

114

give up your pleasures
all your little trivial
sunday school picnics
this is war
in earnest
and red revolution
come in a cloud
with a sun hiding miracle
of small deadly wings
swarm stab and bite
what we want is justice
curses curses curses
over land air and water
whirl in a million
sweeping and swaying
cyclonic dances
whirl high and swoop
down on the cities
like a comet bearing death
in the loop and flick
of its tail
little little creatures
out of all your billions
make great dragons
that lie along the sky
and war with the sunset
and eat up the moon
draw all the poison
from the evil stars
and spit it on the earth
remember every planet
pivots on an atom
and so you are strong

i swear by the great
horned toad of mithridates
i swear by the vision
of whiskered old pythagoras
that i am very angry
i am mad as hell
for i have seen a soapy
kitchen mechanic
murdering my brothers
slaying little roaches
pathetic in their innocence
damn her red elbows
damn her spotted apron
damn her steamy hair
damn her dull eyes
that look like a pair
of little pickled onions
curses curses curses
i even heard her praised
for undertaking murder
on her own volition
and called the only perfect
cook in the city
come come come
come in your billions
tiny small feet
and humming little wings
crawlers and creepers
wigglers and stingers
scratchers borers slitherers
little forked tongues
man is at your mercy
one sudden gesture

and all his empires perish
rise
strike for freedom
curses on the species
that invented roach poison
curses on the stingy
beings that evolved
tight zinc covers
that you can t crawl under
for their garbage cans
come like a sandstorm
spewed from the mouth
of a great apocalyptic
descrt making devil
come like the spray
sooty and fiery
snorted from the nostrils
of a sky eating ogre
let us have a little
direct action is the
sincere wish of

            archy

xxxii

the hen and the oriole

well boss did it
ever strike you that a
hen regrets it just as
much when they wring her
neck as an oriole but
nobody has any
sympathy for a hen because
she is not beautiful
while every one gets
sentimental over the
oriole and says how
shocking to kill the
lovely thing this thought
comes to my mind
because of the earnest
endeavour of a
gentleman to squash me
yesterday afternoon when i
was riding up in the
elevator if i had been a
butterfly he would have
said how did that
beautiful thing happen to
find its way into
these grimy city streets do
not harm the splendid
creature but let it

fly back to its rural
haunts again beauty always
gets the best of
it be beautiful boss
a thing of beauty is a
joy forever
be handsome boss and let
who will be clever is
the sad advice
of your ugly little friend

                    archy

xxxiii

ghosts

you want to know
whether i believe in ghosts
of course i do not believe in them
if you had known
as many of them as i have
you would not
believe in them either
perhaps i have been
unfortunate in my acquaintance
but the ones i have known
have been a bad lot
no one could believe in them
after being acquainted with them
a short time
it is true that i have met
them under peculiar
circumstances
that is while they
were migrating into the
bodies of what human beings
consider a lower order
of creatures
before i became a cockroach
i was a free verse poet
one of the pioneers of the artless art
and my punishment for that
was to have my soul

enter the body of a cockroach
the ghosts i have known
were the ghosts of persons
who were waiting for a vacant
body to get into
they knew they were going
to transmigrate into the bodies of
lizards lice bats snakes
worms beetles mice alley cats
turtles snails tadpoles
etcetera
and while they were waiting
they were as cross as all get out
i remember talking to one of them
who had just worked his way
upward again he had been in the
body of a flea and he was going
into a cat fish
you would think he might be
grateful for the promotion
but not he
i do not call this much of an advance
he said why could i not
be a humming bird or something
kid i told him it will
take you a million years to work your
way up to a humming bird
when i remember he said
that i used to be a hat check boy
in a hotel i could
spend a million years weeping
to think that i should come to this
we have all seen better days i said

we have all come down in the world
you have not come down as far
as some of us
if i ever get to be a hat check boy
again he said i will sting
somebody for what i have had to suffer
that remark will probably cost you
another million years among
the lower creatures i told him
transmigration is a great thing
if you do not weaken
personally my ambition is to get
my time as a cockroach shortened for
good behaviour and be promoted
to a revenue officer
it is not much of a step up but
i am humble
i never ran across any of this
ectoplasm that sir arthur
conan doyle tells of but it sounds
as if it might be wonderful
stuff to mend broken furniture with

                              archy

xxxiv

archy hears from mars

at eleven o clock
p m on last saturday evening
i received the following
message on my
own private radio set
good evening little archibald
and how are you
this is mars speaking
i replied at once
whom or who
as the case may be
do i know on mars
every one here is familiar
with your work archy
was the answer
and we feel well repaid
for all the trouble we have had
in getting in touch
with your planet
thank you i replied
i would rather hear
mars say that
than any other planet
mars has always been
one of my favourite planets
it is sweet of you
to think that way about us

123

said mars
and so we continued to pay
each other interstellar
compliments
what is or are
thirty five million miles
between kindred souls
tell us all about
your planet said mars
well i said it is
round like an orange
or a ball
and it is all cluttered
up with automobiles
and politicians
it doesn t know where it is
going nor why
but it is in a hurry
it is in charge of a
two legged animal called
man who is genuinely
puzzled as to whether
his grandfather was a god
or a monkey
i should think said mars
that what he is himself
would make more difference
than what his grandfather was
not to this animal i replied
he is the great alibi ike of
the cosmos when he raises hell
just because he feels like
raising hell

he wants somebody to blame it on
can t anything be done about him
said mars
i am doing the best i can
i answered
but after all i am only one
and my influence is limited
you are too modest archy
said mars
we all but worship you
here on this planet
a prophet said i is not
without honour save on his own
planet wait a minute
said mars
i want to write that down
that is one of your best things
archy is it original
it was once i answered truthfully
and may be again
won t you tell us a little
something said mars
about yourself what you look like
and what you think
is the best thing you have written
and your favourite games
and that sort of thing
well i said i am brunette
and stand over six feet
without any shoes on
the best skits i have done
were some little plays
i dashed off

under the general title
of shakespeare s plays
and my favourite sport is theology
you must meet
a great many interesting people
said mars
oh yes i said one becomes
accustomed to that after a while
what is your favourite dish
said mars and do you believe
in the immortality of the soul
stew i said and yes
at least mine is immortal
but i could name several others
that i have my doubts about
is there anything else
of interest about your planet
which you wish to tell your
many admirers on mars
asked mars
there is very little else
of any real interest i said
and now will you tune out
and let me do some work
you people who say you admire
my work are always butting in
and taking up my time
how the hell can i get any
serious literary work done
if you keep bothering me
all the time now you get off
the ether and let me do some
deep thinking

you might add that i am shy
and loathe publicity
                              archy

XXXV

mehitabel dances with boreas

well boss i saw mehitabel
last evening
she was out in the alley
dancing on the cold cobbles
while the wild december wind
blew through her frozen whiskers
and as she danced
she wailed and sang to herself
uttering the fragments
that rattled in her cold brain
in part as follows

whirl mehitabel whirl
spin mehitabel spin
thank god you re a lady still
if you have got a frozen skin

blow wind out of the north
to hell with being a pet
my left front foot is brittle
but there s life in the old dame yet

dance mehitabel dance
caper and shake a leg
what little blood is left
will fizz like wine in a keg

wind come out of the north
and pierce to the guts within
but some day mehitabel s guts
will string a violin

moon you re as cold as a frozen
skin of yellow banan
that sticks in the frost and ice
on top of a garbage can

and you throw a shadow so chilly
that it can scarcely leap
dance shadow dance
you ve got no place to sleep

whistle a tune north wind
on my hollow marrow bones
i ll dance the time with three good feet
here on the alley stones

freeze you bloody december
i never could stay a pet
but i am a lady in spite of hell
and there s life in the old dame yet

whirl mehitabel whirl
f lirt your tail and spin
dance to the tune your guts will cry
when they string a violin

eight of my lives are gone
it s years since my fur was slicked

but blow north wind blow
i m damned if i am licked

girls we was all of us ladies
we was o what the hell
and once a lady always game
by crikey blood will tell

i might be somebody s pet
asleep by the fire on a rug
but me i was always romantic
i had the adventurous bug

caper mehitabel caper
leap shadow leap
you gotto dance till the sun comes up
for you got no place to sleep

i might have been many a tom cat s wife
but i got no regret
i lived my life as i liked my life
and there s pep in the old dame yet

blow wind out of the north
you cut like a piece of tin
slice my guts into fiddle strings
and we ll have a violin

spin mehitabel spin
you had a romantic past
and you re gonna cash in dancing
when you are croaked at last

i will not eat tomorrow
and i did not eat today
but wotthehell i ask you
the word is toujours gai

whirl mehitabel whirl
i once was a maltese pet
till i went and got abducted
and cripes i m a lady yet

whirl mehitabel whirl
and show your shadow how
tonight its dance with the bloody moon
tomorrow the garbage scow

whirl mehitabel whirl
spin shadow spin
the wind will pipe on your marrow bones
your slats are a mandolin

by cripes i have danced the shimmy
in rooms as warm as a dream
and gone to sleep on a cushion
with a bellyful of cream

it s one day up and next day down
i led a romantic life
it was being abducted so many times
as spoiled me for a wife

dance mehitabel dance
till your old bones fly apart

i ain t got any regrets
for i gave my life to my art

whirl mehitabel whirl
caper my girl and grin
and pick at your guts with your frosty feet
they re the strings of a violin

girls we was all of us ladies
until we went and fell
and once a thoroughbred always game
i ask you wotthehell

it s last week up and this week down
and always the devil to pay
but cripes i was always the lady
and the word is toujours gai
and the word is toujours gai

be a tabby tame if you want
somebody s pussy and pet
the life i led was the life i liked
and there s pep in the old dame yet

whirl mehitabel whirl
leap shadow leap
you gotto dance till the sun comes up
for you got no place to sleep

archy

xxxvi

archy at the zoo

the centipede adown the street
goes braggartly with scores of feet
a gaudy insect but not neat

the octopus s secret wish
is not to be a formal fish
he dreams that some time he may grow
another set of legs or so
and be a broadway music show

oh do not always take a chance
upon an open countenance
the hippopotamus s smile
conceals a nature full of guile

human wandering through the zoo
what do your cousins think of you

i worry not of what the sphinx
thinks or maybe thinks she thinks

i have observed a setting hen
arise from that same attitude
and cackle forth to chicks and men
some quite superfluous platitude

serious camel sad giraffe

133

are you afraid that if you laugh
those graceful necks will break in half

a lack of any mental outlet
dictates the young cetacean s spoutlet
he frequent blows like me and you
because there s nothing else to do

when one sees in the austral dawn
a wistful penguin perched upon
a bald man's bleak and desert dome
one knows tis yearning for its home

the quite irrational ichneumon
is such a fool it s almost human

despite the sleek shark s far flung grin
and his pretty dorsal fin
his heart is hard and black within
even within a dentist s chair
he still preserves a sinister air
a prudent dentist always fills
himself with gas before he drills

archy

xxxvii

the dissipated hornet

well boss i had a
great example of the corrupting
influence of the great
city brought to my notice recently a
drunken hornet blew in here
the other day and sat down in the
corner and dozed and buzzed not a
real sleep you know one of those wakeful
liquor trances with the
fuzzy talk oozing out of it to hear
this guy mumble in his dreams he was right
wicked my name he says is crusty bill
i never been licked and i never will and
then he would go half way asleep
again nobody around here wanted to
fight him and after a while he got
sober enough to know how drunk he had
been and began to cry over it and get
sentimental about himself mine is a wasted
life he says but i had a good
start red liquor ruined me he says and
sobbed tell me your story i
said two years ago he said i was a country
hornet young and strong and handsome i
lived in a rusty rainspout with my
parents and brothers and sisters and all was
innocent and merry often in that happy

pastoral life would we swoop down
with joyous laughter and sting the school
children on the village green but on an evil
day alas i came to the city in a crate
of peaches i found myself in a market
near the water front alone and friendless in the
great city its ways were strange to
me food seemed inaccessible i thought
that i might starve to death as i was buzzing
down the street thinking these gloomy
thoughts i met another hornet
just outside a speakeasy kid he says
you look down in the mouth forget
it kid i will show you how to live without
working how i says watch me he says just
then a drunken fly came crawling out
of the bar room in a leisurely way my new
found friend stung dissected and consumed that fly
that s the way he says smacking his lips
this is the life that was a beer fly
wait and i will get you a cocktail fly this
is the life i took up that life alas the
flies around a bar room get so drunk drinking
what is spilled that they are helpless all a
hornet has to do is wait calmly until
they come staggering out and there is his
living ready made for him at first being
young and innocent i ate only beer flies but
the curse of drink got me the mad life began
to tell upon me i got so i would not eat a
fly that was not full of some strong and heady
liquor the lights and life got me i would
not eat fruits and vegetables any more i scorned

136

flies from a soda fountain
they seemed flat and insipid to me
finally i got so wicked that i
went back to the country and got six innocent
young hornets and brought them back
to the city with me i started them in the
business i debauched them and
they caught my flies for me now i am in
an awful situation my six hornets from the
country have struck and set up on their own
hook i have to catch my flies myself
and my months of idleness and
dissipation have spoiled my technique i
can t catch a fly now unless he is dead drunk
what is to become of me alas the curse
of alcoholic beverages especially with each
meal well i said it is a sad story
bill and of a sort only too
common in this day of ours it is he says i
have the gout in my stinger so bad
that i scream with pain every time i spear
a fly i got into a safe place on the
inside of the typewriter and yelled out at him
my advice is suicide bill all the time
he had been pitying himself my sympathy had
been with the flies

archy

xxxviii

unjust

poets are always asking
where do the little roses go
underneath the snow
but no one ever thinks to say
where do the little insects stay
this is because
as a general rule
roses are more handsome
than insects
beauty gets the best of it
in this world
i have heard people
say how wicked it was
to kill our feathered
friends
in order to get
their plumage and pinions
for the hats of women
and all the while
these same people
might be eating duck
as they talked
the chances are
that it is just as discouraging
to a duck to have
her head amputated
in order to become

a stuffed roast fowl
and decorate a dining table
as it is for a bird
of gayer plumage
to be bumped
off the running board of existence
to furnish plumage
for a lady s hat
but the duck
does not get the sympathy
because the duck
is not beautiful
the only insect
that succeeds in getting
mourned is a moth
or butterfly
whereas every man s
heel is raised against
the spider
and it is getting harder
and harder for spiders
to make an honest living
at that since
human beings have invented
so many ways
of killing flies
humanity will shed poems
full of tears
over the demise of
a bounding doe
or a young gazelle
but the departure of a trusty
camel leaves the

vast majorities
stonily indifferent
perhaps the theory is
that god would not have made
the camel so ugly
if the camel were not wicked
alas exclamation point
the pathos of ugliness
is only perceived
by us cockroaches of the world
and personally
i am having to stand for a lot
i am getting it double
as you might say
before my soul
migrated into the body
of a cockroach
it inhabited the carcase
of a vers libre poet
some vers libre poets are beautiful
but i was not
i had a little blond moustache
that every one thought was a mistake
and yet since i have died
i have thought of that
with regret
it hung over a mouth
that i found it difficult to keep closed
because of adenoidal trouble
but it would have been better
if i could have kept it closed
because the teeth within
were out of alignment

and were of odd sizes
this destroyed my acoustics
as you might say
my chin was nothing much
and knew it
and timidly shrank
into itself
receding from the battle of life
my eyes were all right
but my eyebrows
were scarcely noticeable
i suppose though that if
i had had noticeable eyebrows
they would have been wrong
somehow
well well not to pursue
this painful subject
to the uttermost and ultimate
wart and freckle
i was not handsome and it hampered
me when i was a human
it militated against me
as a poet
more beautiful creatures could
write verse worse than mine
and get up and recite it
with a triumphant air
and get away with it
but my sublimest ideas
were thought to be a total
loss when people saw
where they came from
i think it would have been

only justice
if i had been sent to inhabit
a butterfly
but there is very little
justice in the universe
what is the use
of being the universe
if you have to be just
interrogation point
and i suppose the universe
had so much really important
business on hand
that it finds it impossible
to look after the details
it is rushed
perhaps it has private
knowledge to the effect
that eternity is brief
after all
and it wants to get the big
jobs finished in a hurry
i find it possible to forgive
the universe
i meet it in a give and take spirit
although i do wish
that it would consult me at times
please forgive
the profundity of these
meditations
whenever i have nothing
particular to say
i find myself always
always plunging into cosmic

archy and mehitabel

**philosophy
or something**

archy

xxxix

the cheerful cricket

i can t see for the
life of me what there is
about crickets that makes people
call them jolly they
are the parrots of the insect race
crying cheer up cheer up
cheer up over and
over again till you want to
swat them i hate one of these
grinning skipping smirking
senseless optimists worse
than i do a cynic or a
pessimist there was
one in here the other day i was
feeling pretty well
and pleased with the world when
he started that confounded
cheer up cheer up cheer up stuff
fellow i said i am
cheerful enough or i was till
a minute ago but you
get on my nerves it s all right
to be bright and merry
but what s the use
pretending you have more
cheerfulness than there is in the
world you sound

insincere to me you insist on
it too much you make
me want to sit in
a tomb and listen to the
screech owls telling
ghost stories to the tree toads i
would rather that i heard a door squeak have
you only one record the sun
shone in my soul today before
you came and you
have made me think of the
world s woe groan
once or i will go mad your
voice floats around the world like
the ghost of a man
who laughed himself to death
listening to funny stories
the boss told i listen to you
and know why shakespeare
killed off mercutio so
early in the play it is only
hamlet that can
find material for five acts
cheer up cheer up cheer up he
says bo i told him i
wish i was the
woolworth tower i would fall
on you cheer up cheer up cheer
up he says again

                              archy

xl

clarence the ghost

the longer i live the more i
realize that everything is
relative even morality is
relative things you would not do
sometimes you would do other
times for instance i would not consider
it honourable in me as a
righteous cockroach to crawl into a
near sighted man s soup that
man would not have a sporting chance but
with a man with ordinarily good eye
sight i should say it was
up to him to watch his soup himself and
yet if i was very tired and hungry
i would crawl into even a near
sighted man s soup knowing all the
time it was wrong and my necessity would
keep me from reproaching myself too
bitterly afterwards you can
not make any hard and fast rule
concerning the morality of crawling into
soup nor anything else a certain
alloy of expediency improves the
gold of morality and makes
it wear all the longer consider a
ghost if i were a ghost i
would not haunt ordinary people but i

would have all the fun i wanted to with
spiritualists for spiritualists are
awful nuisances to ghosts i knew a
ghost by the name of clarence one
time who hated spiritualists with a
great hatred you see said clarence they
give me no rest they have got my
number once one of those psychics gets a
ghost s number so he has to come
when he is called they work him till
the astral sweat stands out in beads
on his spectral brow they seem to think
said clarence that all a spook has to do
is to stick around waiting to dash in
with a message as to whether mrs millionbucks
pet pom has pneumonia or only wheezes
because he has been eating too many
squabs clarence was quite
bitter about it but wait he says till
the fat medium with the red nose
that has my number
passes over and i can get my
clutches on him on equal terms there s
going to be some initiation beside
the styx several of the boys are
sore on him a plump chance i have
don t i to improve myself and pass on
to another star with that medium
yanking me into somebody s parlour to
blow through one of these little tin
trumpets any time of the day or night
honest archy he says i hate the sight of a
ouija board would it be moral he

says to give that goof a bum tip on the
stock market life ain t worth
dying he says if you ve got to fag
for some chinless chump of a psychic
nor death ain t worth living
through would it be moral in me to
queer that simp with his
little circle by saying he s got an
anonymous diamond brooch in his pocket
and that his trances are rapidly developing
his kleptomania no clarence i said it
wouldn t be moral but it
might be expedient there s a ghost
around here i have been trying to get
acquainted with but he is shy i think he is
probably afraid of cockroaches

                    archy

xli

some natural history

the patagonian
penguin
is a most
peculiar
bird
he lives on
pussy
willows
and his tongue
is always furred
the porcupine
of chile
sleeps his life away
and that is how
the needles
get into the hay
the argentinian
oyster
is a very
subtle gink
for when he s
being eaten
he pretends he is
a skink
when you see
a sea gull
sitting

on a bald man s dome
she likely thinks
she s nesting
on her rocky
island home
do not tease
the inmates
when strolling
through the zoo
for they have
their finer feelings
the same
as me and you
oh deride not
the camel
if grief should
make him die
his ghost will come
to haunt you
with tears
in either eye
and the spirit of
a camel
in the midnight gloom
can be so very
cheerless
as it wanders
round the room

archy

xlii

prudence

i do not think a prudent one
will ever aim too high
a cockroach seldom whips a dog
and seldom should he try

and should a locust take a vow
to eat a pyramid
he likely would wear out his teeth
before he ever did

i do not think the prudent one
hastes to initiate
a sequence of events which he
lacks power to terminate

for should i kick the woolworth tower
so hard i laid it low
it probably might injure me
if it fell on my toe

i do not think the prudent one
will be inclined to boast
lest circumstances unforeseen
should get him goat and ghost

for should i tell my friends i d drink
the hudson river dry

the archy and mehitabel omnibus

a tidal wave might come and turn
my statements to a lie

archy

xliii

archy goes abroad

london england
since i have been
residing in westminster
abbey i have learned
a secret that i desire
to pass on to the psychic
sharps it is this
until the body of a human
being perishes utterly
the spirit is not
released from its vicinity
so long as there is any
form left in the physical
part of it the ghost can not go
to heaven or to hell
the ancient greeks
understood this and they
burned the body very often
so that the spirit could
get immediate release
the ancient egyptians
also knew it
but they reacted differently
to the knowledge
they embalmed the body
so that the form would
persist for thousands

of years and the ghost would have
to stick around for a time
here in westminster abbey
there are hundreds of
ghosts that have not yet
been released
some of them are able to wander
a few miles away
and some of them cannot
go further than a few hundred
yards from the graves
where the bodies lie
for the most part they make
the best of it
they go out on little
excursions around london
and at night they sit on
their tombs and
tell their experiences
to each other
it is perhaps the most
exclusive club in london
henry the eighth came in
about three o clock this morning
after rambling about
piccadilly for a couple of hours
and i wish i had the
space to report in detail
the ensuing conversation
between him and charles dickens
now and then
a ghost can so influence
a living person that you

might say he had grabbed off
that living person s body and was
using it as his own
edward the black prince
was telling the gang
the other evening
that he had been leading the life
of a city clerk for three weeks
one of those birds
with a top hat and a sack coat
who come floating through
the mist and drizzle
with manuscript cases
under their arms looking unreal
even when they are not animated
by ghosts edward the black prince
who is known democratically
as neddie black here
says this clerk was a mild and
humble wight when he took
him over but he worked
him up to the place where
he assaulted a policeman
saturday night then left him flat
one of the most pathetic
sights however
is to see the ghost of queen
victoria going out every
evening with the ghost
of a sceptre in her hand
to find mr lytton strachey
and bean him it seems she beans
him and beans him and he

never knows it
and every night on the stroke
of midnight elizabeth tudor
is married to walter raleigh by that
eminent clergyman
dr lawrence sterne
the gang pulls a good many
pageants which are written
by ben jonson but i think
the jinks will not be properly
planned and staged until
j m barrie gets here
this is the jolliest bunch
i have met in london
they have learned
since they passed over
that appearances and suety
pudding are not all they were
cracked up to be more anon from your little friend

archy

xliv

archy at the tomb of napoleon

paris france
i went over to
the hotel des invalides
today and gazed on
the sarcophagus of the
great napoleon
and the thought came
to me as i looked
down indeed it
is true napoleon
that the best goods
come in the smallest
packages here are
you napoleon with
your glorious course
run and here is
archy just in the
prime of his career
with his greatest
triumphs still before
him neither one of us
had a happy youth
neither one of us
was welcomed socially at
the beginning of his
career neither one of
us was considered much

to look at
and in ten thousand years from
now perhaps what you said and did
napoleon will be
confused with what
archy said and did
and perhaps the burial
place of neither will be
known napoleon looking
down upon you
i wish to ask you now
frankly as one famous
person to another
has it been worth
all the energy
that we expended all the
toil and trouble and
turmoil that it cost us
if you had your life
to live over
again bonaparte would
you pursue the star
of ambition
i tell you frankly
bonaparte that i myself
would choose the
humbler part
i would put the temptation
of greatness aside
and remain an ordinary
cockroach simple
and obscure but alas
there is a destiny that

pushes one forward
no matter how hard
one may try to resist it
i do not need to
tell you about that
bonaparte you know as
much about it as i do
yes looking at it in
the broader way neither
one of us has been to blame
for what he has done
neither for his great
successes nor his great mistakes
both of us napoleon
were impelled by some
mighty force external to
ourselves we are both to
be judged as great forces of
nature as tools in the
hand of fate rather than as
individuals who willed to
do what we have done
we must be forgiven
napoleon
you and i
when we have been
different from the common
run of creatures
i forgive you as i know
that you would forgive
me could you speak to me
and if you and i
napoleon forgive and

understand each other
what matters it if all
the world else find
things in both of us that
they find it hard
to forgive and understand
we have been
what we have been
napoleon and let them laugh that off
well after an hour or so of
meditation there i left
actually feeling that i
had been in communion
with that great spirit and
that for once in my
life i had understood and been
understood
and i went away feeling
solemn but likewise
uplifted mehitabel the
cat is missing
                                archy

xlv

mehitabel meets an affinity

paris france
mehitabel the cat
has been passing her
time in the dubious
company of
a ragged eared tom cat
with one mean
eye and the other
eye missing whom
she calls francy
he has been the hero
or the victim of
many desperate encounters
for part of his tail
has been removed
and his back has been chewed
to the spine
one can see at a glance
that he is a sneak thief
and an apache
a bandit with long
curved claws
you see his likes hanging
about the outdoor markets
here in paris waiting
their chance to sneak
a fish or a bit

of unregarded meat
or whimpering
among the chair legs at the
sidewalk cafes in the
evenings or slinking
down the gutters of
alleys in the old
quarters of the town
he has a raucous voice
much damaged by the night
air and yet there is a
sentimental wheedling
note in it as well
and yet withal he carries
his visible disgrace with
a jaunty air
when i asked mehitabel
where in the name of st denis
did you pick up that
romantic criminal
in the luxembourg gardens
she replied where
we had both gone to kill
birds he has been showing me
paris he does not
understand english but speak of
him with respect
he is like myself
an example of the truth
of the pythagorean idea
you know that in my body
which is that of a cat
there is reincarnated

the soul of cleopatra
well this cat here
was not always a cat either
he has seen better days
he tells me that once he was
a bard and lived here in paris
tell archy here
something about yourself francy
thus encouraged the
murderous looking animal spoke
and i append a
rough translation of
what he said

tame cats on a web of the persian woof
may lick their coats and purr for cream
but i am a tougher kind of goof
scheming a freer kind of scheme
daily i climb where the pigeons gleam
over the gargoyles of notre dame
robbing their nests to hear them scream
for i am a cat of the devil i am

i ll tell the world i am a hard boiled oeuf
i rend the clouds when i let off steam
to the orderly life i cry pouf pouf
it is worth far less than the bourgeois deem
my life is a dance on the edge de l abime
and i am the singer you d love to slam
who murders the midnight anonyme
for i am a cat of the devil i am

when the ribald moon leers over the roof

and the mist reeks up from the chuckling stream
i pad the quais on a silent hoof
dreaming the vagabond s ancient dream
where the piebald toms of the quartier teem
and fight for a fish or a mouldy clam
my rival i rip and his guts unseam
for i am a cat of the devil i am

roach i could rattle you rhymes by the ream
in proof of the fact that i m no spring lamb
maybe the headsman will finish the theme
for i am a cat of the devil i am

mehitabel i said
your friend is nobody else
than francois villon
and he looks it too

archy

xlvi

mehitabel sees paris

paris france
i have not been
to geneva but i have been
talking to a french cockroach
who has just returned
from there travelling all the
way in a third class
compartment he says there is no
hope for insect or man in
the league of nations
what prestige it ever had is gone
and it never had any
the idea of one great brotherhood
of men and insects on earth
is very attractive to me
but mehitabel the cat
says i am a communist an
anarchist and a socialist
she has been shocked to the soul
she says by what the
revolutionists did here during
the revolution
i am always the aristocrat archy
she said i may go and play
around montmartre and that sort
of thing and in fact i was
playing up there with francy last

night but i am always the lady
in spite of my little larks
toujours gai archy and toujours
the lady that is my motto in
spite of
ups and downs
what they did to us aristocrats
at the time of the revolution
was a plenty archy
it makes my heart bleed
to see signs of it all
over town those poor
dear duchesses that got it
in the neck i can sympathize
with them archy i may not
look it now but i come of a
royal race myself
i have come down in the world
but wotthehell archy wotthehell
jamais triste archy jamais triste
that is my motto
always the lady and always
out for a good time
francy and i lapped up
a demi of beer in a joint
up on the butte last night
that an american tourist
poured out for us
and everybody laughed and it
got to be the fashion up there
to feed beer to us cats
i did not get a vulgar souse
archy no lady gets a vulgar

souse wotthehell i hope i am above
all vulgarity but i did get a
little bit lit up
and francy did too we came
down and got on top of the
new morgue and sang and did
dances there
francy seems to see
something attractive about
morgues when he gets lit up
the old morgue he says was
a more romantic morgue but
vandal hands have torn it down
but wotthehell archy this one
will do to dance on
francy is showing me a side of
paris he says tourists don t often
get a look at he has a little
love nest down in the
catacombs where
he and i are living now
he and i go down there
and do the tango amongst the
bones he is really a most
entertaining and agreeable
companion archy and he has some
very quaint ideas he is busy now
writing a poem about
us two cats filled with beer
dancing among the bones
sometimes i think francy
is a little morbid
when i see these lovely old places

that us aristocrats built archy
in the hands of the bourgeois it
makes me almost wild
but i try to bear up i try
to bear up i find agreeable
companions and put a good face
on it toujours gai that is my
motto toujours gai
francy is a little bit done up
today he tried to steal a
partridge out of a frying
pan in a joint up on the butte
we went back there for more beer
after our party
at the morgue
and the cook beaned him with
a bottle poor francy i
should hate to lose him
but something tells me i should
not stay a widow long
there is something in the air
of paris archy
that makes one young again
there s more than one
dance in the old dame yet
and with these words she
put her tail in the air and
capered off down the alley
i am afraid we shall never
get mehitabel back to america

                    archy

xlvii

mehitabel in the catacombs

paris france
i would
fear greatly for the morals
of mehitabel the cat if she had any
the kind of life she
is leading is too violent
and undisciplined for words
she and the disreputable
tom cat who claims to have
been francois villon
when he was on earth
before have taken up their
permanent abode in the catacombs
whence they sally
forth nightly on excursions
of the most undignified nature
sometimes they honour
with their presence the cafes
of montparnasse and the boul mich
and sometimes they
seek diversion in the cabarets
on top of the butte
of montmartre
in these localities
it has become the fashion
among the humans
to feed beer to these

peculiar cats and they dance
and caper when they have
become well alcoholized
with this beverage
swinging their tails and
indulging in raucous feline
cries which they evidently
mistake for a song
it was my dubious
privilege to see them
when they returned to their
abode early yesterday morning
flushed as you might say
with bocks and still
in a holiday mood
the catacombs of paris are
not lined with the bones
of saints and martyrs
as are those of rome
but nevertheless these cats
should have more respect
for the relics of mortality
you may not believe me
but they actually danced and
capered among
the skeletons while the cat
who calls himself
francois villon gave forth
a chant of which the following
is a free translation

outcast bones from a thousand biers
click us a measure giddy and gleg

and caper my children dance my dears
skeleton rattle your mouldy leg
this one was a gourmet round as a keg
and that had the brow of semiramis
o fleshless forehead bald as an egg
all men s lovers come to this
this eyeless head that laughs and leers
was a chass daf once or a touareg
with golden rings in his yellow ears
skeleton rattle your mouldy leg
marot was this one or wilde or a wegg
who dropped into verses and down the abyss
and those are the bones of my old love meg
all men s lovers come to this

these bones were a ballet girl s for years
parbleu but she shook a wicked peg
and those ribs there were a noble peer s
skeleton rattle your mouldy leg

and here is a duchess that loved a yegg
with her lipless mouth that once drank bliss
down to the dreg of its ultimate dreg
all men s lovers come to this

prince if you pipe and plead and beg
you may yet be crowned with a grisly kiss
skeleton rattle your mouldy leg
all men s lovers come to this

archy

xlviii

off with the old love

paris france
i think
mehitabel the cat and the
outcast feline
who calls himself francois
villon are about to
quarrel and separate
mehitabel is getting tired
of living in the catacombs
she said to me
last evening
archy i sometimes wish
that francy s gaiety
did not so frequently take
a necrological turn
when francy is really happy
he always breaks
into a series of
lyric epitaphs
personally archy
i am a lady who can
be gay outside of
a mausoleum
as for morgues
and cemeteries i can
take them or i can
leave them alone

just because some of my
ancestors are now mummies
i do not feel
that i have to wait
till i see a sarcophagus
before i cheer up
i can fall in love
with a gentleman friend without
speculating how he is going
to look to the undertaker
and when i want to sing
a comic song
i do not always feel
impelled to hunt up a tomb
for a stage
i am a lady of refinement
archy i have had my ups
and downs and i have made
a few false steps in life
but i am toujours la grande dame
archy always the lady
old kid to hell with anything
coarse or unrefined
that has always been my motto
and the truth is that this
francy person has a yellow
streak of commonness
running through his poetic nature
i fell for him archy
but i feel there is trouble
coming we had words last
night over something no real
gentleman would have noticed

and the slob said to me
mehitabel if you make eyes again
at that tortoise shell
cat over there i will slice
your eyes out
with a single sweep of my claws
and toss them to the pigeons
archy those are words
that no gentleman would use
or no lady would take
you piebald fish thief
i told him
if i were not too refined
i would rip you
from the gullet to the mid riff
it is lucky for you
you frog eating four flush
that i always remember
my breeding
otherwise you would be
a candidate for what they call
civet stew in paris
something I won t stand for in a
gentleman friend
is jealousy of every other
person who may be attracted to me
by my gaiety and
aristocratic manner
and if i hear another word
out of you
i will can you first
and kill you afterwards
and then i will ignore you

archy a gentleman
with any real spirit
would have swung on me
when i said that
but this quitter let me
get away with it
i clawed him a little archy
just to show him i could
and the goof stood for it
no cat can hold me archy
that lets me claw him without
a come back i am a strong free
spirit and i live my own
life and only a masterful
cave cat can hold my affections
he must be a gentleman
but he must also make me feel
that he could be a
wild cat if he would
this francy person is neither
one nor the other
ah me archy i am afraid
my little romance
is drawing to a close
and no meal ticket in sight
either but what the hell archy
a lady can always find friends
it won t be the first time
i have been alone in the world
toujours gai archy
that is my motto
there s more than one dance
in the old dame yet

      archy

archys life of mehitabel

Archy the Cockroach made his initial appearance in my office a good many years ago, in fact about the same time that free verse began to commend itself to the multitudes because it looked as if it would be so easy to write. There was a period which many persons still more or less alive may remember when you could not scratch a taxi-driver, an insurance agent, or a newspaper reporter without finding a free-verse poet under the skin. Archy claimed that he was a victim of transmigration; that he had been a *vers libre* bard, and that for his sins of omission and commission his soul had been sentenced to serve an indeterminate sentence in the body of a cockroach. Mehitabel the Cat, who appeared about the same time, made a similar claim; before she was Mehitabel, she said, she had been Cleopatra and various other lively ladies.

Archy writes without punctuation because he is forced to use his head to butt the keys of the typewriter one at a time, and he is not able to reach the shift keys of the machine in order to make punctuation marks or capital letters. Mehitabel does not use the typewriting machine at all, so Archy is forced to be her reporter.

DON MARQUIS

contents

i

the life of mehitabel the cat

boss i am engaged on a literary
work of some importance it is
nothing more nor less
than the life story of
mehitabel the cat she is
dictating it a word
at a time and all
the bunch gather around to listen but
i am rewriting it as i go along
boss i wish we
could do something
for mehitabel she is
a cat that has seen
better days she has
drunk cream at fourteen
cents the half pint
in her time and now she
is thankful for a
stray fish head from a
garbage cart but she is
cheerful under it all toujours
gai is ever her word
toujours gai kiddo drink she
says played a great
part in it all she
was taught to drink
beer by a kitchen maid she

trusted and was
abducted from a luxurious home
on one occasion in a
taxicab while under
the influence of beer which
she feels certain had been
drugged but still her
word is toujours gai my
kiddo toujours gai wotto hell
luck may change

archy

ii

the minstrel and the maltese cross

well boss i promised to tell you
something of the life story of
mehitabel the cat archy says she i
was a beautiful kitten and as good
and innocent as i was beautiful my
mother was an angora you dont
look angora i said your fur
should show it did
i say angora said mehitabel it must
have been a slip of the tongue my
mother was high born and of
ancient lineage part persian and part
maltese a sort of maltese cross
i said archy she said please
do not josh my mother i
cannot permit levity in connection
with that saintly name she knew many
troubles did my mother and
died at last in a slum far from
all who had known her in her better
days but alas my father
was a villain he too had noble blood
but he had fallen into dissolute
ways and wandered the
alleys as the leader of a troupe of
strolling minstrels stealing milk
from bottles in the early mornings

catching rats here there and
everywhere and only too frequently
driven to the expedient of dining on
what might be found in
garbage cans and suburban
dump heaps now and
then a sparrow or a robin fell to my
fathers lot for he was a mighty hunter i
have heard that at times he even
ate cockroaches and as she said
that she spread
her claws and looked at me with her
head on one side i got into the works
of the typewriter mehitabel i
said try and conquer that wild and
hobohemian strain in your blood archy
she said have no fear i have dined
today but to resume my
mother the pampered beauty that she
was was eating whipped cream one
day on the back
stoop of the palace where she resided
when along came my father bold
black handsome villain that he was and
serenaded her his must have been a
magnetic personality for in spite of
her maiden modesty and
cloistered upbringing she responded
with a few well rendered musical
notes of her own i
will not dwell upon the wooing suffice
it to say that ere long they
not only sang duets together but

she was persuaded to join
him and his troupe of strollers in
their midnight meanderings alas that
first false step she
finally left her luxurious home it was
on a moonlight night in may i have
often heard her say and again and
again she has said to me that she
wished that robert w chambers could
have written her story or maybe john
galsworthy in his later and
more cosmopolitan manner well to
resume i was born in a stable in
greenwich village which was at
the time undergoing transformation
into a studio my
brothers and sisters were drowned
dearie i often look back on my life and
think how romantic it has all
been and wonder what fate saved
me and sent my brothers and sisters
to their watery grave archy i
have had a remarkable life go
on telling about it i said never
mind the side remarks i became
a pet at once continued
mehitabel but let us not make the first
instalment too long the
tale of my youth will be reserved
for your next chapter to be continued

archy

187

iii

mehitabels first mistake

well i said to
mehitabel the cat continue
the story of your life i
was a pampered kitten for
a time archy she said but
alas i soon
realized that my master and
mistress were becoming
more and more fond of a
dog that lived with
them in the studio he was
an ugly mutt take it from
me archy a red eyed little bull
dog with no manners i
hope i was too much of a lady
to show jealousy i have
been through a great deal
dearie now up and now down
but it is darn seldom
i ever forget i was a
lady always genteel archy
but this red eyed mutt was
certainly some pill and those
people were so stuck on
him that it would have made
you sick they called him
snookums and it was snookums

this and snookums that and
ribbons and bells and porterhouse
steak for him and if he
got a flea on him they called a
specialist in only one
day archy i hear my
mistress say snookums ookums
is lonely he ought to
have some one to play with
true said her husband every
dog should be brought up along
with a baby a dog
naturally likes a child to
play with we will have no
children said she a
vulgar foolish little child
might harm my snookums we
could muzzle the child said
her husband i am sure
the dog would like one to
play with and they
finally decided they would get
one from a foundling home
to play with snookums if
they could find a child
with a good enough pedigree
that wouldnt give any
germs to the dog well
one day the low lived mutt
butted in and tried to
swipe the cream i was drinking even
as a kitten archy i
never let any one put anything

across on me although i
am slow in starting
things as any real lady
should be dearie i let
this stiff snookums get
his face into the saucer
and then what i did
to his eyes and nose with
my claws would melt the
heart of a trained
nurse the simp had no
nerve he ran to his
mistress and she came after
me with a broom i
got three good scratches
through her silk stockings
archy dearie before i
was batted into the
alley and i picked myself
up out of a can full
of ashes a cat without a
home a poor little
innocent kitten alone
all alone in the great and
wicked city but i never
was one to be down
on my luck long archy my
motto has always been
toujours gai archy toujours
gai always jolly archy
always game and thank god
always the lady i
wandered a block or

archys life of mehitabel

two and strayed into
the family entrance of
a barroom it was my
first mistake mehitabels
adventures will be continued

archy

iv

the curse of drink

to continue the story
of mehitabel the cat
she says to me when i
walked into that
barroom i was hungry and
mewing with despair
there were two men sitting
at the table and
looking sad i rubbed
against the legs of one
of them but he never moved
then i jumped up on
the table and stood
between them they both stared
hard at me and
then they stared at each
other but neither one
touched me or said anything
in front of one of
them was a glass full
of some liquid with
foam on the top of it i
thought it was milk
and began to drink from the
glass little did i
know archy as i lapped
it up that it was beer the

men shrank back from me and
began to tremble and shake
and look at me
finally one of them said to
the other i know what you
think bill what do i
think jeff said the
other you think bill that
i have the d ts said the
first one you think i
think i see a cat drinking
out of that beer glass but
i do not think i
see a cat at all that is all
in your imagination it
is you yourself that
have the d ts no said the
other one i dont think
you think you see a
cat i was not thinking
about cats at all i
do not know why you mention
cats for there are no
cats here just then a
salvation army lassic came
in and said you
wicked men teaching that poor
little innocent cat to
drink beer what cat
said one of the men she
thinks she sees a cat
said the other and
laughed and laughed

just then a mouse ran
across the floor and i
chased it and the salvation
lassie jumped on a
chair and screamed jeff
said bill i suppose now you
think i saw a
mouse i wish bill you
would change the
subject from animals said
jeff there is nothing
to be gained by talking
of animals mehitabels
life story will be
continued in an early number

                archy

V

pussy café

for some weeks said
mehitabel the cat continuing the
story of her life i
lived in that barroom and
though the society was
not what i had
been used to yet i
cannot say that it was
not interesting three
times a day in
addition to scraps from
the free lunch
and an occasional mouse
i was given a saucer
full of beer sometimes i
was given more and
when i was feeling
frolicsome it was the custom
for the patrons to gather
round and watch me
chase my tail until
i would suddenly fall
asleep at that time
they gave me the
nickname of pussy café but
one day i left the
place in the pocket

of a big fur
overcoat worn by
a gentleman who was
carrying so much that i thought
a little extra burden would
not be noticed he got
into a taxi cab
which soon afterwards
pulled up in front of
a swell residence uptown
and wandered up the
steps well said his
wife meeting him in the
hallway you are here
at last but where is my
mother whom i sent you to
the train to meet
could this be she asked
the ladys husband
pulling me out of his
coat pocket by the neck and
holding me up with a
dazed expression on his face
it could not said his
wife with a look of
scorn mehitabels life
story will be continued
before long
                              archy

vi

a communication from archy

well boss i am
sorry to report that
mehitabel the cat has
struck no more story archy
she said last night
without pay art for arts
sake is all right but
i can get real
money in the movies the
best bits are to
come too she says my life
she says has been a
romantic one boss she has
the nerve to hold out
for a pint of
cream a day i am sick
of milk she says and
why should a lady author
drink ordinary milk cream
for mine she says
and no white of egg beaten
up on top of it either i
know what my dope
is worth boss it is
my opinion she has the
swell head over getting into
print i would hate

to stop the serial
but she needs a
lesson listen archy she said
to me what i want
with my stuff is
illustrations too the next
chapter is about me taking
my first false step well
archy i either get an
illustration for that or else
i sign up with these
movie people who are always
after me you will be
wanting to sing into a phonograph
next i told her
my advice is to
can her at once i will fill
the space with my own
adventures

                                archy

vii

the return of archy

where have i been so long
you ask me
i have been going up
and down like the devil
seeking what i might devour
i am hungry always hungry
and in the end i shall
eat everything
all the world shall come at
last to the multitudinous maws
of insects
a civilization perishes
before the tireless teeth
of little little germs
ha ha i have thrown off the mask
at last
you thought i was only
an archy
but i am more than that
i am anarchy
where have i been you ask
i have been organizing the insects
the ants the worms the wasps
the bees the cockroaches
the mosquitoes
for a revolt against mankind
i have declared war

upon humanity
i even i shall f ling
the mighty atom
that splits a planet asunder
i ride the microbe
that crashes down olympus
where have i been you ask me where
i am jove and from my seat
on the edge of a bowl of beef stew
i launch the thunderous
molecule
that smites a cosmos into bits
where have i been you ask
but you had better ask
who follows in my train
there is an ant
a desert ant a tamerlane
who ate a pyramid in rage
that he might get at and devour
the mummies of six hundred
kings who in remote
antiquity had stepped upon
and crushed ascendants of his
my myrmidons
are trivial things
and they have always ruled
the world
and now they shall strike down mankind
i shall show you how
a solar system
pivots on the nubbin
of a flageolet bean
i shall show you how a blood clot

moving in a despots brain
flung a hundred million men
to death and disease
and plunged a planet into woe
for twice a hundred years
we have the key
to the fourth dimension
for we know the little things
that swim and swarm
in protoplasm
i can show you love and hate
and the future
dreaming side by side
in a cell
in the little cells where
matter is so fine it merges
into spirit
you ask me where i have been
but you had better
ask me where i am
and what
i have been drinking
exclamation point

                                archy

viii

archy turns highbrow for a minute

boss please let me
be highbrow for
a minute i
have just been eating
my way through some of
the books on your desk
and i have digested two of them
and it occurs to me
that antoninus the emperor
and epictetus the slave
arrived at the same
philosophy of life
that there is neither mastery
nor slavery
except as it exists
in the attitude of the soul
toward the world
thank you for listening
to a poor little
cockroach
archy

ix

archy experiences a seizure

'Where have you been so long? And what on earth do you mean by coming in here soused?' we asked Archy as he zigzagged from the door to the desk.

He climbed onto the typewriter keys and replied indignantly:

> soused yourself i havent had a drink
> and yet i am elevated i admit it i have
> been down to a second hand book
> store eating a lot of kiplings earlier
> poetry it always excites me if i eat
> a dozen stanzas of it i get all lit up
> and i try to imitate it get out of my
> way now i feel a poem in the kipling
> manner taking me

And before we could stop him he began to butt on the keys:

> the cockroach stood by the mickle
>   wood in the flush of the astral dawn

We interrupted. 'Don't you mean Austral instead of astral?'

Archy became angered and wrote peevishly:

> i wrote astral and i meant astral

you let me be now i want to get this
poem off my chest you are jealous if
you were any kind of a sport at all
you would fix this machine so i could
write it in capitals it is a poem about
a fight between a cockroach and a
lot of other things get out of my way
im off

the cockroach stood by the mickle
    wood in the flush of the astral dawn
and he sniffed the air from the hidden
    lair where the khyber swordfish spawn
and the bilge and belch of the glutton
    welsh as they smelted their warlock cheese
surged to and fro where the grinding
    floe wrenched at the headlands knees
half seas over under up again
and the barnacles white in the moon
the pole stars chasing its tail like a pup again
and the dish ran away with the spoon

the waterspout came bellowing out of
    the red horizons rim
and the grey typhoon and the black
    monsoon surged forth to the fight with him
with three fold might they surged to
    the fight for they hated the great bull roach
and they cried begod as they lashed
    the sod and here is an egg to poach
we will bash his mug with his own raw
    lug new stripped from off his dome
for there is no law but teeth and claw

to the nor nor east of nome
the punjab gull shall have his skull
   ere he goes to the burning ghaut
for there is no time for aught but crime
   where the jungle lore is taught
across the dark the afghan shark is
   whining for his head
there shall be no rule but death and
   dule till the deep red maws are fed
half seas under up and down again
and her keel was blown off in a squall
girls we misdoubt that we ll ever see town again
haul boys haul boys haul.

'Archy,' we interrupted, 'that haul, boys, is all right to the
eye, but the ear will surely make it hall boys. Better change
it.'

   you are jealous you let me alone im off again

the cockroach spat and he tilted his
   hat and he grinned through the lowering mirk
the cockroach felt in his rangoon belt
   for his good bengali dirk
he reefed his mast against the blast
   and he bent his mizzen free
and he pointed the cleats of his bin
   nacle sheets at the teeth of the yesty sea
he opened his mouth and he sluiced
   his drouth with his last good can of swipes
begod he cried they come in pride but
   they shall go home with the gripes

begod he said if they want my head it
  is here on top of my chine
it shall never be said that i doffed my
  head for the boast of a heathen line
and he scorned to wait but he dared
  his fate and loosed his bridle rein
and leapt to close with his red fanged
  foes in the trough of the screaming main
from hell to nome the blow went home
  and split the firmament
from hell to nome the yellow foam
  blew wide to veil the rent
and the roaring ships they came to
  grips in the gloom of a dripping mist

'Archy,' we interrupted again, 'is there very much more of it? It seems that you might tell in a very few words now who won the fight, and let it go at that. Who did win the fight, Archy?'

But Archy was peeved, and went sadly away, after writing:

of course you wont let me finish i never saw as jealous a person as you are

X

peace – at a price

one thing the human
bean never seems to
get into it is the
fact that humans
appear just as unnecessary to
cockroaches as cockroaches
do to humans
you would scarcely
call me human
nor am i altogether
cockroach i
conceive it to be my
mission in life to bring
humans and cockroaches
into a better understanding
with each other to
establish some sort of
entente cordiale or
hands across the kitchen sink
arrangement
lately i heard a number
of cockroaches discussing
humanity one big
regal looking roach
had the floor and he spoke
as was fitting in blank verse
more or less

says he
how came this monster with the heavy
foot harsh voice and cruel heart to
rule the world
had it been dogs or cats or elephants
i could have acquiesced and found a
justice working in the decree but man
gross man
the killer man the bloody minded
crossed unsocial death dispenser of this
sphere who slays for pleasure slays
for sport for whim
who slays from habit breeds to slay and
slays
whatever breed has humors not his own
the whole apparent universe one sponge
blood filled from insect mammal fish
and bird
the which he squeezes down his vast
gullet friends i call on you to rise and
trample down this monster man this
tyrant man hear hear said
several of the wilder spirits
and it looked to me for a
minute as if they
were going right out and
wreck new york city but
an old polonius looking
roach got the floor
he cleared his throat three times
and said
what our young friend here
so eloquently counsels against

the traditional enemy is
calculated of course to appeal to
youth what he says
about man is all very true
and yet we must remember that
some of our wisest
cockroaches have always
held that there
is something impious in the
idea of overthrowing man
doubtless the supreme being
put man where he is and
doubtless he did it
for some good purpose which
it would be very
impolitic yea well nigh
blasphemous for us to enquire
into the project of
overthrowing man is indeed
tantamount to a
proposition to overthrow the
supreme being himself and
i trust that no one of
my hearers is so wild or
so wicked as to think
that possible or desirable i
cannot but admire the
idealism and patriotism of
my young friend who
has just spoken nor do i
doubt his sincerity but i
grieve to see so
many fine qualities

misdirected and i
should like to ask him
just one question to wit
namely as follows is it not
a fact that just before
coming to this meeting
he was almost killed by a
human being as he
crawled out of an ice box
and is it not true that
he was stealing food from
the said ice box and is it
not a fact that his own
recent personal experience has
as much to do with
his present rage as any
desire to better the
condition of the cockroaches of
the world in general
i think that it is the sense of
this meeting that a
resolution be passed censuring
mankind and at the
same time making it
very clear that nothing like
rebellion is to be attempted
and so on
well polonius had his way
but it is my belief that the
wilder spirits will gain the
ascendancy and if the
movement spreads to the other
insects the human race is in

danger as a friend of both
parties i should regret war
what we need is
intelligent propaganda who is
better qualified to handle
the propaganda fund than
yours truly
                        archy

xi

mehitabel again

well boss mehitabel the
cat is sore at me she says
that it was my fault
that you cut off her story
of her life right in
the middle and she
has been making my life a
misery to me three
times she has almost clawed
me to death i wish
she would eat a poisoned
rat but she wont she
is too lazy to catch one well
it takes all sorts of
people to make an
underworld

archy

xii

archy among the philistines

i wish i had more human society
these other cockroaches here are just cockroaches
no human soul ever transmigrated into them
and any soul that would go into one of them
after giving them the once over
would be a pretty punk sort of a soul
you cant imagine how low down they are with no
esthetic sense and no imagination or anything like
that and they actually poke fun at me because i used to
be a poet before i died and my soul migrated into a
cockroach they are as crass and philistine as some
humans i could name their only thought is food but
there is a little red eyed spider lives behind your
steam radiator who has considerable sense
i dont think he is very honest though i dont know
whether he has anything human in him or is just
spider i was talking to him the other day and was
quite charmed with his conversation
after you he says pausing by the radiator
and i was about to step back of the radiator ahead
of him when something told me to watch my step
and i drew back just in time
to keep from walking into a web
there were some cockroach legs and wings
still sticking in that web
i beat it as quickly as i could up the wall
well well says that spider you are in quite a hurry archy

haa so you wont be at my dinner table today then
some other time cockroach some other time
i will be glad to welcome you to dinner archy
he is not to be trusted but he is the only insect
i have met for weeks that has any intelligence if you
will look back of that locker where you hang your
hat you will find a dime has rolled there i wish you
would get it and spend it for doughnuts a cent at a time
and leave the doughnuts under your typewriter i get
   tired
of apple peelings i nearly drowned in your ink well last
night dont forget the doughnuts

                               archy

We are trying to fix up some scheme whereby Archy can use the shift keys and thus get control of the capital letters and punctuation marks. Suggestions for a workable device will be thankfully received. As it is Archy has to climb upon the frame of the typewriter and jump with all his weight upon the keys, a key at a time, and it is only by almost incredible exertions that he is able to drag the paper forward so he can start a new line.

214

xiii

archy protests

say comma boss comma capital
i apostrophe m getting tired of
being joshed about my
punctuation period capital t followed by
he idea seems to be
that capital i apostrophe m
ignorant where punctuation
is concerned period capital n followed by
o such thing semi
colon the fact is that
the mechanical exigencies of
the case prevent my use of
all the characters on the
typewriter keyboard period
capital i apostrophe m
doing the best capital
i can under difficulties semi colon
and capital i apostrophe m
grieved at the unkindness
of the criticism period please
consider that my name
is signed in small
caps period

                    archy period

xiv

CAPITALS AT LAST

I THOUGHT THAT SOME HISTORIC DAY
SHIFT KEYS WOULD LOCK IN SUCH A WAY
THAT MY POETIC FEET WOULD FALL
UPON EACH CLICKING CAPITAL
AND NOW FROM KEY TO KEY I CLIMB
TO WRITE MY GRATITUDE IN RHYME
YOU LITTLE KNOW WITH WHAT DELIGHT
THROUGHOUT THE LONG AND LONELY NIGHT
I'VE KICKED AND BUTTED (FOOT AND BEAN)
AGAINST THE KEYS OF YOUR MACHINE
TO TELL THE MOVING TALE OF ALL
THAT TO A COCKROACH MAY BEFALL
INDEED IF I COULD NOT HAVE HAD
SUCH OCCUPATION I'D BE MAD
AH FOR A SOUL LIKE MINE TO DWELL
WITHIN A COCKROACH THAT IS HELL
TO SCURRY FROM THE PLAYFUL CAT
TO DODGE THE INSECT EATING RAT
THE HUNGRY SPIDER TO EVADE
THE MOUSE THAT %) ?))" " " $$$ ((gee boss
what a jolt that cat mehitabel made
a jump for me
i got away but she unlocked the shift key
it kicked me right into the
mechanism where she
couldn't reach me it
was nearly the death of little

216

archy that kick spurned me right
out of parnassus back into
the vers libre slums i lay
in behind the wires for an hour after
she left before i dared to get
out and finish i hate
cats say boss please lock the shift
key tight some night
i would like to tell the story of
my life all in capital
letters

                              archy

XV

the stuff of literature

thank your friends for me for
all their good advice about how to
work your typewriter but what i have
always claimed is that manners and methods
are no great matter compared
with thoughts in poetry you cant hide
gems of thought so they wont flash
on the world on the other hand if you press
agent poor stuff that wont make it live
my ego will express itself in spite of
all mechanical obstacles having something
to say is the thing being sincere
counts for more than forms of expression thanks
for the doughnuts
                              archy

xvi

archys autobiography

if all the verse what i have wrote
were boiled together in a kettle
twould make a meal for every goat
from nome to popocatapetl
mexico

and all the prose what i have penned
if laid together end to end
would reach from russia to south bend
indiana

but all the money what i saved
from all them works at which i slaved
is not enough to get me shaved
every morning

and all the dams which i care
if heaped together in the air
would not reach much of anywhere
they wouldnt

because i dont shave every day
and i write for arts sake anyway
and always hate to take my pay
i loathe it

and all of you who credit that

could sit down on an opera hat
and never crush the darn thing flat
you skeptics

                archy

xvii

quote and only man is vile quote

as a representative
of the insect world
i have often wondered
on what man bases his claims
to superiority
everything he knows he has had
to learn whereas we insects are born
knowing everything we need to know
for instance man had to invent
airplanes before he could fly
but if a fly cannot fly
as soon as he is hatched
his parents kick him out and disown him
i should describe the human race
as a strange species of bipeds
who cannot run fast enough
to collect the money
which they owe themselves
as far as government is concerned
men after thousands of years practice
are not as well organized socially
as the average ant hill or beehive
they cannot build dwellings
as beautiful as a spiders web
and i never saw a city
full of men manage to be as happy
as a congregation of mosquitoes

who have discovered a fat man
on a camping trip
as far as personal beauty
is concerned who ever saw
man woman or child
who could compete with a butterfly
if you tell a dancer
that she is a firefly
she is complimented
a musical composer
is all puffed up with pride
if he can catch the spirit
of a summer night full of crickets
man cannot even make war
with the efficiency and generalship
of an army of warrior ants
and he has done little else
but make war for centuries
make war and wonder
how he is going to pay for it
man is a queer looking gink
who uses what brains he has
to get himself into trouble with
and then blames it on the fates
the only invention man ever made
which we insects do not have
is money and he gives up
everything else to get money
and then discovers that it is not worth
what he gave up to get it
in his envy he invents
insect exterminators
but in time every city he builds

is eaten down by insects
what i ask you is babylon now
it is the habitation of fleas
also ninevah and tyre
humanitys culture consists
in sitting down in circles
and passing the word around
about how darned smart humanity is
i wish you would tell
the furnace man at your house
to put out some new brand
of roach paste i do not get
any kick any more out of the brand
he has been using the last year
formerly it pepped me up
and stimulated me
i have a strange tale about
mehitabel to tell you
more anon

                    archy

xviii

mehitabels morals

boss i got
a message from
mehitabel the cat
the other day
brought me by
a cockroach
she asks for our help
it seems she is being
held at ellis
island while an
investigation is made
of her morals
she left the country
and now it looks as
if she might not
be able to get
back in again
she cannot see
why they are
investigating
her morals she says
wotthehellbill she says
i never claimed
i had any morals
she has always regarded
morals as an unnecessary
complication in life

her theory is
that they take up room that might
better be devoted to
something more interesting
live while you are alive
she says and postpone
morality to the hereafter
everything in its place
is my rule she says
but i am liberal she
says i do not give
a damn how moral other
people are i never try
to interfere with them
in fact i prefer them
moral they furnish
a background for my
vivacity in the meantime
it looks as if she
would have to swim
if she gets ashore and
the water is cold

                              archy

xix

cream de la cream

well boss mehitabel the cat
has turned up again after a long
absence she declines
to explain her movements but she
drops out dark hints of a
most melodramatic nature ups and downs
archy she says always ups and downs
that is what my life has
been one day lapping
up the cream de la cream and the
next skirmishing for
fish heads in an alley but
toujours gai archy toujours gai no
matter how the luck broke i have had a
most romantic life archy talk
about reincarnation and transmigration
archy why i could tell you things of who
i used to be archy that would make
your eyes stick out like a snails one
incarnation queening it with a tarara on
my bean as cleopatra archy and
the next being abducted as a poor
working girl but toujours gai archy toujours
gai and finally my soul has migrated to
the body of a cat and not even a persian or
a maltese at that but where have you been

lately mehitabel i asked her never mind
archy she says dont ask no questions
and i will tell no lies all i
got to say is keep away
from the movies have you been in the
movies mehitabel i asked her never mind
archy she says never mind all i got to
say is keep away from those
movie camps theres some mighty
nice people and animals connected with them
and then again theres some that aint i
say nothing against anybody archy i am
used to ups and downs no matter
how luck breaks its toujours gai
with me all i got to say
archy is that sometimes a cat
comes along that is a perfect gentleman and
then again some of the slickest furred ones
aint if i was a cat that was the
particular pet of a movie star archy and
slept on a silk cushion and had
white chinese rats especially
imported for my meals i would try to live
up to all that luxury and be a
gentleman in word and deed mehitabel i said
have you had another unfortunate romance i am
making no complaint against any
one archy she says wottell archy wottell even
if the breaks is bad my motto is toujours gai
but to slip out nights and sing and frolic
under the moon with a lady and then cut her
dead in the day time before your rich

friends and see her batted out of a studio
with a broom without raising a paw for her
aint what i call being a
gentleman archy and i am
a lady archy and i know a gentleman when
i meet one but wottell archy wottell toujours
gai is the word never say die
archy its the cheerful heart that wins all i
got to say is that if i ever get that
fluffy haired slob down on the
water front when some of my gang
is around he will wish he had
watched his step i aint vindictive archy i
dont hold grudges no lady does but i
got friends archy that maybe would take it
up for me theres a black cat with one ear
sliced off lives down around old slip is a
good pal of mine i wouldnt want to
see trouble start archy no real lady
wants a fight to start over her but
sometimes she cant hold her friends back
all i got to say is that boob with his silver
bells around his neck better sidestep old slip
well archy lets not talk any more about my troubles
does the boss ever leave any pieces of sandwich
in the waste paper basket any more honest
archy i would will myself to a furrier for a
pair of oysters i could even she says eat you
archy she said it like a joke but there
was a kind of a pondering look in her eyes
so i just crawled into the inside of
your typewriter behind the wires it
seemed safer let her hustle for a

mouse if she is as hungry as all that
but i am afraid she never will she
is too romantic to work

      archy

XX

do not pity mehitabel

do not pity
mehitabel
she is having
her own kind of
a good time
in her own way
she would not
understand any other
sort of life
but the life
she has chosen
to lead
she was predestined
to it as the
sparks fly upward
chacun à son gout
as they say in france
start her in
as a kitten
and she would
repeat the same story
and do not overlook
the fact that
mehitabel is really
proud of herself
she enjoys
her own sufferings

archy

xxi

mehitabel tries companionate marriage

boss i have seen mehitabel the cat
again and she has just been through
another matrimonial experience
she said in part as follows
i am always the sap archy
always the good natured simp
always believing in the good intentions
of those deceitful tom cats
always getting married at leisure
and repenting in haste
its wrong for an artist to marry
a free spirit has gotta
live her own life
about three months ago along came a
maltese tom with a black heart and
silver bells on his neck and says
mehitabel be mine
are you abducting me percy i asks him
no said he i am offering marriage
honorable up to date
companionate marriage
listen i said if its marriage
theres a catch in it somewheres
ive been married again and again
and its been my experience
that any kind of marriage
means just one dam kitten after another

and domesticity always ruins my art
but this companionate marriage says he
is all assets and no liabilities
its something new mehitabel
be mine mehitabel and i promise
a life of open ice boxes
creamed fish and catnip
well i said wotthehell kid
if its something new i will take a
chance theres a dance or two
in the old dame yet
i will try any kind of marriage once
you look like a gentleman to me percy
well archy i was wrong as usual
i wont go into details for i aint
any tabloid newspaper
but the way it worked out was i rustled
grub for that low lived bum for two
months and when the kittens came
he left me flat and he says these
offsprings dissolves the wedding
i am always the lady archy
i didn t do anything vulgar
i removed his left eye with one claw
and i says to him if i wasn t an
aristocrat id rip you
from gehenna to duodenum
the next four flusher that
says marriage to me
i may really lose my temper
trial marriage or companionate
marriage or old fashioned american
plan three meals a day marriage

archys life of mehitabel

with no thursdays off
they are all the same thing
marriage is marriage
and you cant laugh that curse off

archy

xxii

no social stuff for mehitabel

i said to mehitabel
the cat i suppose you are
going to the swell cat
show i am not archy
said she i have as
much lineage as any
of those society
cats but i never could
see the conventional
social stuff archy
i am a lady
but i am bohemian
too archy i
live my own life
no bells and pink
ribbons for me
archy it is me for
the life romantic i could
walk right into
that cat show and get
away with it
archy none of those
maltese princesses has
anything on me in the
way of hauteur
or birth either or any
of the aristocratic

fixings and condiments
that mark the
cats of lady clara
vere de vere but
it bores me archy
me for the
wide open spaces the
alley serenade and
the moonlight
sonata on the back
fences i would
rather kill my own
rats and share
them with a
friend from greenwich
village than lap up
cream or beef juice
from a silver porringer
and have to
be polite to the
bourgeois clans
that feed me
wot the hell i
feel superior to that
stupid bunch me
for a dance
across the roofs when
the red star
calls to my blood
none of your
pretty puss stuff for
mehitabel it would
give me a grouch

to have to be so
solemn toujours
gai archy toujours
gai is my
motto

                    archy

xxiii

the open spaces are too open

boss i saw mehitabel
the cat yesterday she is
back in town after
spending a couple
of weeks
in the country
archy she says to me
i will never leave the
city again no
matter what the weather
may be me for the
cobble stones and the
asphalt and the friendly
alleys the great open
spaces are all right but
they are too open i have been
living on a diet of
open spaces the country is
all right if you have a trained
human family to rustle
up the eats for you or know
a cow who has the
gift of milking herself for
your benefit but archy
i am a city lady
i was never educated to dig for
field mice and as for calling

birds out of the trees i dont
have the musical
education for it i cant
even imitate a cat bird
i will take my chance
hereafter with the garbage
cans in town until
such times as i decorate
a rubbish heap myself
that may not be long archy
but wot the hell
i have had a good time while
i lasted come easy go easy
archy that is my motto
i tried to snatch a bone
from a terrier a month
ago and the beast bit my front
paw nearly off
but wot the hell archy
wot the hell i can still
dance a merry step or two
on three legs i am
slightly disabled archy but
still in the ring and still
i have the class wot the
hell archy i am always
a lady and always gay
and i got one eye out of
that terrier at that
i would be afraid that
mehitabel s end is not far off
if she had not been looking
as bad as she does for

at least three years
she says it is her
romantic disposition
that keeps her young
and yet i think if some
cheerful musical family
in good circumstances were to
offer mehitabel a home
where she would be treated in
all ways as one of the family
she has reached the point where
she might consent to give up
living her own life
only three legs archy she says
to me only three legs left
but wot the hell archy
there s a dance in the old
dame yet

                                archy

xxiv

random thoughts by archy

one thing that
shows that
insects are
superior to men
is the fact that
insects run their
affairs without
political campaigns
elections and so forth

a man thinks
he amounts to a lot
but to a mosquito
a man is
merely
something to eat

i have noticed
that when
chickens quit
quarrelling over their
food they often
find that there is
enough for all of them
i wonder if
it might not
be the same way

with the
human race

germs are very
objectionable to men
but a germ
thinks of a man
as only the swamp
in which
he has to live

a louse i
used to know
told me that
millionaires and
bums tasted
about alike
to him

the trouble with
most people is
that they
lose their sense of
proportion
of what use is
it for a
queen bee to fall in
love with a bull

what is all this mystery
about the sphinx
that has troubled so many
illustrious men

no doubt the very same
thoughts she thinks
are thought every day
by some obscure hen

                    archy

XXV

archy turns revolutionist

if all the bugs
in all the worlds
twixt earth and betelgoose
should sharpen up
their little stings
and turn their feelings loose
they soon would show
all human beans
in saturn
earth
or mars
their relative significance
among the spinning stars
man is so proud
the haughty simp
so hard for to approach
and he looks down
with such an air
on spider
midge
or roach
the supercilious silliness
of this poor wingless bird
is cosmically comical
and stellarly absurd
his scutellated occiput
has holes somewhere inside

and there no doubt
two pints or so
of scrambled brains reside
if all the bugs
of all the stars
should sting him on the dome
they might pierce through
that osseous rind
and find the brains at home
and in the convolutions lay
an egg with fancies fraught
which
germinating rapidly
might turn into a thought
might turn into the thought
that men
and insects are the same
both transient flecks
of starry dust
that out of nothing came
the planets are
what atoms are
and neither more nor less
man s feet have grown
so big that he
forgets his littleness
the things he thinks
are only things
that insects always knew
the things he does
are stunts that we
don t have to think to do
he spent a score

of centuries
in getting feeble wings
which we instinctively
acquired
with other trivial things
the day is coming
very soon
when man and all his race
must cast their silly
pride aside
and take the second place
i ll take the bugs
of all the stars
and tell them of my plan
and fling them with
their myriad stings
against the tyrant man
dear boss this outburst
is the result
of a personal insult
as so much verse always is
maybe you know how
that is yourself
i dropped into an irish
stew in a restaurant
the other evening
for a warm bath and a bite
to eat and a low browed
waiter plucked me out
and said to me
if you must eat i will
lead you to the
food i have especially prepared

for you and he took me
to the kitchen
and tried to make me
fill myself with
a poisonous concoction
known cynically as roach food
can you wonder
that my anger
against the whole human
race has blazed forth in
song when the revolution
comes i shall
do my best to save
you you have so many
points that are far
from being human

                              archy

xxvi

archys last name

boss i just discovered what
my last name is i
pass it on to you i belong to the
family of the blattidae right o
said mehitabel the cat when i told her
about it they have
got you sized up right you blatt out
everything you hear
i gleaned the information from
a bulletin issued by the
united states department of
agriculture which you left on the
floor by your desk it was entitled
cockroaches and written by
e l marlatt entomologist and acting
chief in the absence of the chief and he
tells a dozen ways of killing roaches boss
what business has the united states
government got
to sick a high salaried
expert onto a poor little roach
please leave me some
more cheerful literature also please
get your typewriter fixed the keys are
working hard again butting them as i
do one at a time with
my head i get awful pains in my

neck writing for you
                    archy

248

xxvii

quote buns by great men quote

one of the most
pathetic things i
have seen recently
was an intoxicated person
trying to fall
down a moving stairway
it was the escalator at
the thirty fourth street
side of the
pennsylvania station
he could not fall down as
fast as it
carried him up again but
he was game he kept on
trying he was
stubborn about it
evidently it was a part of
his tradition habit and
training always to fall down
stairs when intoxicated and
he did not intend to
be defeated this time i
watched him for an hour
and moved sadly away thinking
how much sorrow
drink is responsible for the
buns by great men

reached and kept
are not attained
by sudden f light but they
while their companions slept
were falling upwards
through the night

           archy

xxviii

archys song

man eats the big fish
the big fish eat the
little fish
the little fish
eat insects
in the water
the water insects
eat the water plants
the water plants
eat mud
mud eats man
my favorite poem
is the same as
abraham lincolns
o why should the spirit
of mortal be proud
awaiting your answer
i am and so forth

archy

xxix

an awful warning

dear boss i was walking along
the curbstone yesterday
and i ran sprang into an old bum
who was sitting happily
in the gutter singing
in part as follows

oh i ruined my prospects
by wicked desires
which i put into action
as far as i could
but now i ve arrived
within sight of hell fires
and i wish i d done better
i wish i d been good

as i sit in the gutter
and look at the sky
the man in the moon
is a looking at me
and i thinks to myself
i d have risen that high
if i had behaved myself
proper as he

now all you young fellows
and pretty young janes

as passes me by
and dont pitch me a dime
take warning by me
and avoid all the pains
which comes from remorse
in the fullness of time

and all you young fellows
thats out on a bust
and lively young flappers
so spic and so span
i oncet had a sweetheart
and me she did trust
to maintain myself always
a proper young man

i was lured to a barroom
and there i was tempted
for the bartender cried
be a man and drink rum
and after that first
glass of liquor i emptied
i found myself jobless
and went on the bum

now all you young fellows
and flappers so gay
that passes me by
and dont toss me a cent
there oncet was a time
when i went on my way
with ladylike janes
like an elegant gent

now i sits in the gutter
and looks at the stars
and wish i had always
behaved and been good
and never drunk rum
at them elegant bars
and never been wicked
as much as i could

you gents and your girl friends
should tip an old man
for his horrid example
of not being good
you must try and behave
in so far as you can
you should toss me a dime
for my warning you should

                              archy

XXX

as it looks to archy

ants go on their cheerful way
merrily from day to day
building cities out of sand
and they seem to understand
dwelling therein peacefully
disciplined and orderly
and the much lauded bee contrives
for to fill his thundering hives
with a ranked society
based on work and honesty
and a thousand neat examples
could i cite of insect lives
free from much that tears and tramples
human beings and their wives
even the coral in the ocean
throughout his dim and damp existence
scorns political commotion
and labours with a glad persistence
worthy of large commendations
to erect his naval stations

man the universal simp
follows lagging with a limp
treading on his neighbours toes
the way the little insect goes
in a million years or more
man may learn the simple lore

of how the bees are organized
and why the ants are civilized
may even hope for to approach
the culture of an average roach
if he is humble and not smug
may emulate the tumble bug

for we insects now inherit
all humanity has builded
all they raised with brawn and spirit
all the domes and spires they gilded
time the anthropophagous
swallows down all human works
through his broad esophagus
moslems christians hindus turks
pass to their sarcophagus
leaving nothing much on earth
which even beetles find of worth
i mention nineveh and tyre
i cite the tower of babel
troy which fell into the fire
and sodom with its rabble
where are all the towns of siddim
where the kings of crete
long long since the desert hid em
and the spiders bite their feet
following an old convention
dating back to jeremiah
i might even mention
babylon i might enquire
where o where is babylon
and the echo answers where
for its former ruling wizards

sleep in sand and silicon
with gravel in their gizzards
and sand burrs in their hair
and the centipedes are dancing
in the chambers of the palace
where the kings and queens entrancing
used to quaff the ruby chalice
and proceed to their romancing

i look forward to the day
when the human race is done
and we insects romp and play
freely underneath the sun
and no roach paste is scattered
about anywhere i got another jolt of it
last night and today i seem to have a case
of intestinal flu the trouble with you
human beings is you are just plain wicked

archy

xxxi

archy a low brow

boss i saw a picture
of myself in a paper
the other day
writing on a typewriter
with some of my feet
i wish it was as easy
as that what i have to do
is dive at each key
on the machine
and bump it with my head
and sometimes it telescopes
my occiput into my
vertebrae and i have a
permanent callous
on my forehead
i am in fact becoming
a low brow think of it
me with all my learning
to become a low brow
hoping that you
will remain the same
i am as ever your
faithful little bug

                                    archy

xxxii

archy on the radio

dear boss
i hope you tuned in
last evening when mars and i
were on the radio together
our first joint appearance
in several years

do you realize said mars
that next week will be archy week
all over mars
and several other prominent planets

                    archy
good gracious mars it had slipped
my memory

                    mars
do you know that you are
our favorite author here and
we all but worship you

                    archy
well mars as far as that goes
you are one of my favorite planets

                    mars
what a coincidence

archy
the long arm of coincidence
makes many radio connections

mars
is that your own phrase archy

archy
mine until the next air programme
nowadays an author owns his stuff
only between air programmes

mars
did you know about the archy clubs here

archy
i hope they can t throw them this far
what do they look like

mars
like dumbbells ha ha ha
but please tell us how you happened
to start your career as a writer

archy
it did not happen it was something
i planned deliberately so i could quit
being what i was

mars
explain please the stars are listening

archy

well you see i was the four marx brothers
and it became annoying because
i quarrelled among myself all the time
so in order to end it all i turned
author writing dante s inferno and
mehitabel the cat

mars

what do you call that little planet
where you are at

archy

well now what do you call it

mars

we call it goofus

archy

goofus goofus why goofus

mars

not long ago one of our prominent
scientists got a good look at it
with a new fangled telescope and
he laughed himself to death crying out
goofus goofus goofus all the time
he said from the way it looked it couldn t
be named anything else but goofus

archy

well if that s the way you feel who was
the lady i seen you walking with last sunday

                              mars
that wasn t no lady that was venus
is there any particular message
you would like to send your billions
and billions of admirers in these parts

                              archy
oh yes tell them
this hour is by the courtesy
of the knockem cold roach and bug killing company
and that i wish to testify
that their product has several times
brought me personally nearer the great adventure
than any other roach paste i ever ate
i always carry a flask of bath tub gin with me
as an antidote

                              mars
will you describe yourself for your
worshipers here

                              archy
i am over six feet and go everywhere

                              mars
who has influenced you most in a
literary way

                              archy
theodore dreiser and bernard shaw
they taught me how far an author can go
if he never loses patience with himself

                              262

mars

archy it is impossible that you should
not lose patience with yourself sometimes

archy

well i havent gone as far as they have either

mars

what are the conditions of life on your planet archy

archy

they practically dont exist any more

mars

but how do people get along

archy

the men make a living by talking
about how much they have lost
during the depression
and the women and children pick up
what they can by listening
how is it by yourself old timer

mars

we never had to do any work here
we get our living by biting electrons out of the air
which we crack with our teeth
and eat the kernels while we spit
the shells into space which accounts
for a lot of the static you hear

archy

that not only interests me as a scientist
but it seems much more refined than
working for a living

mars

yes it is refined all right but it is
expensive it runs into terrible dentists bills

archy

but dentists bills are always terrible
everywhere anyhow

mars

wait till i write that down please
do you have to think a long time
for those brilliant things
or do they just come to you

archy

i never think at all when i write
nobody can do two things at the same time
and do them both well

mars

are you starting any new literary movements on
your planet

archy

oh yes the latest literary movement
consists in going to all the fences
and coal sheds near all the school houses
and copying off of them all the bad words

written there by naughty little boys
over the week ends
and these form the bases of the new novels
of course these novels are kept away
from the young so they will not be contaminated

mars
but where do the boys get the words

archy
from hired hands and the classics

archy

xxxiii

mehitabels parlour story

boss did you
hear about the two drunks
who were riding in
a ford or something
equally comic
and the ford or
whatever it was nearly
went off the
road one of
the drunks poked the
other and said thickly
they always talk thickly in
these stories
anyway he said hey look
out how youre driving
youll have us in
the ditch in a minute if
you dont look out
why said the second
drunk who was drunker
i thought you
were driving i got
that from mehitabel the
cat its the first parlour
story ive ever heard
her tell and ive known
her for five or six

266

years now

archy

xxxiv

archys mission

well boss i am
going to quit living
a life of leisure
i have been an idler
and a waster and a
mere poet too long
my conscience has waked up
wish yours would do the same
i am going to have
a moral purpose in my life
hereafter and a cause
i am going to reclaim
cockroaches and teach them
proper ways of living
i am going to see if i cannot
reform insects in general
i have constituted
myself a missionary
extraordinary
and minister
plenipotentiary
and entomological
to bring idealism to
the little struggling brothers
the conditions in the insect
world today would shock
american reformers

if they knew about them
the lives they lead
are scarcely fit to print
i cannot go into
details but the contented
laxness in which i find
them is frightful
a family newspaper is no place
for these revelations
but i am trying to have
printed in paris
for limited circulation
amongst truly earnest
souls a volume which will
be entitled
the truth about the insects
i assure you there is nothing
even in the old testament
as terrible
i shall be the cotton mather
of the boll weevil

                              archy

XXXV

archy visits washington

washington d c july
23 well boss here
i am in washington
watching my step for fear
some one will push me
into the food bill up
to date i am the only thing
in this country that
has not been added to it by
the time this is
published nothing that
i have said may be
true however which is a
thing that is constantly happening
to thousands of
great journalists now in
washington it is so hot here that
i get stuck in the asphalt
every day on my
way from the senate press
gallery back to
shoemakers where the
affairs of the nation
are habitually settled by
the old settlers it
is so hot that you can
fry fish on the

sidewalk in any part of
town and many people
are here with fish to fry
including now
and then a german
carp i am lodging on
top of the washington
monument where i can
overlook things
you cant keep a good bug
from the top of
the column all the time i
am taking my meals with
the specimens in the
smithsonian institution when i
see any one coming i hold
my breath and look like another
specimen but in the
capitol building there
is no attention paid to me
because there are so
many other insects
around it gives you a
great idea of the
american people when you
see some of the
things they elect after july
27 address me care
st elizabeth hospital
for the insane i am going out
there for a visit with
some of your other
contributors

                    archy

xxxvi

ballade of the under side

by archy
the roach that scurries
skips and runs
may read far more than those
that fly
i know what family skeletons
within your closets
swing and dry
not that i ever
play the spy
but as in corners
dim i bide
i can t dodge knowledge
though i try
i see things from
the under side

the lordly ones the
haughty ones
with supercilious
heads held high
the up stage stiff
pretentious guns
miss much that meets
my humbler eye
not that i meddle
perk or pry

but i m too small
to feel great pride
and as the pompous world
goes by
i see things from
the under side

above me wheel
the stars and suns
but humans shut
me from the sky
you see their eyes as pure
as nuns
i see their wayward
feet and sly
i own and own it with
a sigh
my point of view
is somewhat wried
i am a pessimistic
guy
i see things from the
under side

l envoi
prince cre you pull a bluff
and lie
before you fake
and play the snide
consider whether
archy s nigh
i see things from
the under side

xxxvii

archy wants to end it all

well boss from time
to time i just simply
get bored with having
to be a cockroach my
soul my real ego if
you get what i mean is
tired of being shut
up in an insects body the
best you can say for it is that it
is unusual and you could
say as much for mumps so
while feeling gloomy the
other night the thought came
to me why not
go on to the next stage as
soon as possible why not
commit suicide and
maybe be reincarnated in
some higher form of life why
not be the captain of my
soul the master of my fate and
the more i pondered over it the
more i was attracted to
the notion well boss you would
be surprised to find
out how hard it is for a
cockroach to commit suicide unless

you have been one
and tried it of course i
could let mehitabel the
cat damage me and die that
way but all my finer sensibilities
revolt at the idea i jumped out
the fourth story window and
a wind caught me and blew
me into the eighth story i
tried to hang myself with a
thread and i am so light i
just swung back and forth and
didnt even choke myself shooting
is out of the question and poison
is not within
my reach i might drown myself
in the ink well but if
you ever got a mouthful of it you
would know it was a
thing no refined person could go
on with boss i am going to
end it all before long and i
want to go easy have you
any suggestion yours
for transmigration

archy

xxxviii

book review

boss a new book
has appeared
which should be
read by every one
it is entitled
the cockroach
its life history
and how to deal
with it and
the author
is frederick laing
who is assistant
in the department
of entomology in the
british museum
of natural history
it is one of the
best books i ever
tasted i am eating
the binding from
a copy with
a great deal of
relish and
recommend it
to all other
insects yours
truly

                archy

xxxix

archy and the old un

one of the saddest
creatures i ever saw
was a turtle who said
he was a thousand
years old
no turtle looks very
joyous the style of
architecture peculiar
to the faces and necks of
turtles is such
that even if they were to
feel gay internally
they would find difficulty
in expressing their joy
a kind of melancholy dwells
in the wrinkles of a
turtles neck the only thing
that looks sadder than a turtle
is the little dead fish
that is served in an italian
tabledhote restaurant
well this turtle i am telling you
about was so old that
he used to be a pet
of charlemagne
and he finally committed suicide
he stood on his hind

legs and jumped up
and bit himself on the
forehead and held on until
he died
i wrote a poem
about this turtle
after his death
which goes as follows
why did he die perhaps he knew
too much about
the ways of men and turtles
he had seen too much no doubt

optimist in youth of course
youth never quails
he preached to all his brother turtles
moral turtles turn to whales

but the weary ages passed
and he perceived
turtles still continued turtles
then he doubted disbelieved

brooding for two hundred years
in discontent
he became a snapping turtle
savage cynic in his bent

timon of the turtle tribe
so he withdrew
from the world remarking often
piffle there is nothing true

nothing changes all the salt
that used to be
scattered widely through the ocean
still gives flavour to the sea

nothing changes all the bunk
of long ago
still is swallowed by the nations
progress always stubs its toe

the moral well the morals quite
an easy one

do not live to be a thousand
youll be sorry ere youre done

the only way boss
to keep hope in the world
is to keep changing its
population frequently
i am sorry to be so
pessimistic today
but you see i need a change
very badly
when do we start
for hollywood
i am eager to be gone
i wish to cheer myself
up in some fashion
your faithful little
cockroach
                    archibald

xl

archygrams

the wood louse sits on a splinter
and sings to the rising sap
aint it awful how winter
lingers in springtimes lap

it is a good
thing not to be too
aristocratic
the oldest and
most pedigreed
families in this
country are the
occupants of various sarcophagi
in the museums
but it is dull associating
with mummies no
matter how royal their
blood used to be when
they had blood
it is like living in
philadelphia

honesty is a good
thing but
it is not profitable to
its possessor
unless it is

kept under control
if you are not
honest at all
everybody hates you
and if you are
absolutely honest
you get martyred

as i was crawling
through the holes in
a swiss cheese
the other
day it occurred to
me to wonder
what a swiss cheese
would think if
a swiss cheese
could think and after
cogitating for some
time i said to myself
if a swiss cheese
could think
it would think that
a swiss cheese
was the most important
thing in the world
just as everything that
can think at all
does think about itself

these anarchists that
are going to
destroy organized

society and civilization
and everything remind
me of an ant i
knew one time
he was a big red ant a
regular bull of an
ant and he came bulging down a
garden path and ran
into a stone gate post curses on
you said the ant to the
stone gate post get out of my
way but the stone never budged
i will kick you over
said the ant and he kicked but
it only hurt his hind legs
well then said
the ant i will eat you down and
he began taking little bites
in a great rage maybe i said
you will do it in
time but it will
spoil your digestion first

a good many
failures are happy
because they don t
realize it many a
cockroach believes
himself as beautiful
as a butterfly
have a heart o have
a heart and
let them dream on

boss i believe
that the
millennium will
get here some day
but i could
compile quite a list
of persons
who will have
to go
first

tis very seldom i have felt
drawn to a scallop or a smelt
and still more rarely do i feel
love for the sleck electric eel

the oyster is useful in his fashion
but has little pride or passion

when the proud ibexes start from sleep
in the early alpine morns
at once from crag to crag they leap
alighting on their horns
and may a dozen times rebound
ere resting haughty on the ground
i do not like their trivial pride
nor think them truly dignified

did you ever
notice that when
a politician
does get an idea

he usually
gets it all wrong

xli

archy says

one queer thing about
spring gardens is
that so many people
use them to
raise spinach in
instead of food

everybody has two kinds of friends
one kind tries to run
his affairs for him
and the other kind
well i will be darned if i can remember
the other kind

now and then
there is a person born
who is so unlucky
that he runs into accidents
which started out to happen
to somebody else

xlii

sings of los angeles

boss i see by
the papers there
has been more than
one unconventional
episode
in the far west
and i have made
a little song
as follows
los angeles
los angeles
the home of the movie star
what kind of angels
are they
out there where you are
los angeles
los angeles
much must be left
untold
but science says
that freuds rush in
where angels
fear to tread
los angeles
los angeles
clean up your
movie game

archys life of mehitabel

or else o city of angels
you better
change your name
yours for all the morality
that the traffic
will bear

                         archy

xliii

wants to go in the movies

boss i wish you would
make arrangements to put me
into the movies a
lot of people who are no
handsomer in the face than i
am are drawing millions of
dollars a year i
have always felt that i
could act if i
were given the chance and a
truly refined cockroach might
be a novelty but do not pay
any attention to the
wishes of mehitabel the cat along
this line mehitabel
told me the other day that several
firms were bidding against
each other for her
services i would be the greatest
feline vamp in the
history of the screen said
mehitabel wot the hell archy
wot the hell ain t i a
reincarnation of cleopatra and
dont the vamp stuff come quite
natural to me i will say it
does but i have refused all

offers archy up to
date they must pay me
my price the
truth is that mehitabel hasnt a
chance and she is not a
steady character by the way
here is a piece of political news
for you mehitabel tells me that
the cats in greenwich
village and the adjoining
neighbourhoods are forming soviets now
they are going in for bolshevism
her soviet she says
meets in washington mews
they are for the nationalization
of all fish markets

archy

xliv

the retreat from hollywood

Archy, the Free Verse Cockroach, and Mehitabel the Cat are on their way back from Hollywood, hitch-hiking. Mehitabel was forcibly ejected at least twice from every moving-picture studio in Hollywood, and nourishes animosity against the art of the cinema. Archy reports that when they left Hollywood Mehitabel and seven platinum-blonde kittens, who were attempting to follow her across the desert . . . but here is the latest bulletin from Archy:

> mehitabels third kitten succumbed
> to a scorpion today
> poor little thing she said
> i suppose the next one will perish
> in a sandstorm and the next one
> fall into the colorado river
> it breaks my heart i am all
> maternal instinct next to my art
> as a modern dancer mother love is
> the strongest thing in me
> it is so strong that sometimes life seems to me
> to be just one damned kitten
> after another
> but of course if i get back to broadway
> without any kittens i will have more
> freedom for my art
> and can live my own life again
> then she began to practice

dance steps among the cactus
casting fond eyes at a coyote

boss i am afraid
that mehitabels morals are no better
than before she struck hollywood
after all she remarked kittens
are but passing episodes in the life
of a great artist i may have been
given the bums rush from six auto camps
in three days but hells bells
i am still a lady

the loss of that kitten is a terrible grief
but an aristocrat and an artist
must bear up toujours gai
is my motto toujours gai

theres life in the old dame yet
and with that she cut a caper with
the heat at one hundred and forty
degrees fahrenheit

xlv

artists shouldnt have offspring

A bulletin from Archy the Cockroach, who started out last July to hitch-hike from Hollywood to New York with Mehitabel the Cat and Mehitabel's seven platinum-blonde kittens:

had a great break boss
got a ride on the running board of a car
and caught up with mehitabel
in new mexico where she is gadding about
with a coyote friend
i asked her where the kittens were
kittens said mehitabel kittens
with a puzzled look on her face
why goodness gracious i seem to remember
that i did have some kittens
i hope nothing terrible has happened
to the poor little things but if something has
i suppose they are better off
an artist like me shouldnt really
have offspring it handicaps her career
archy i want you to meet my boy friend
cowboy bill the coyote i call him
i am trying to get him to come to new york
with me and do a burlesque turn
isnt he handsome i said tactfully that he looked
very distinguished to me and all bill said
was nerts insect nerts
                                    archy

xlvi

what does a trouper care

A bulletin from Archy, who started weeks ago hitch-hiking across the country from California to New York, accompanied by Mehitabel and the seven platinum-blonde kittens she acquired in Hollywood:

        still somewhere in arizona
        sometime in october
        sand storm struck us yesterday
        i peeped out from under a rock
        and saw mehitabel dancing
        and singing as follows
        ive got a rock in my eye
        and a scorpion in my gizzard
        but what does an artist care
        for a bit of red hot blizzard
        my feet are full of cactus
        there are blisters in my hair
        but howl storm howl
        what does a trouper care
        i got a thirst like a mummy
        i got a desert chill
        but cheerio my deario
        theres a dance in the old dame still
        two more of the kittens disappeared
        well i got three left said mehitabel
        poor little dears i am afraid
        they will never reach broadway

unless they learn how to get milk
from the cactus plants damn them
their appetites are spoiling my figure
a lot of encouragement a dancer gets
from her family i must-say
any other artist i know would tell them
to go wean themselves on alkali
and be done with them but my great weakness
is my maternal instinct
boss i made nearly a mile today
before the sand storm blew me back
i hear texas is a thousand miles across

                    archy

xlvii

is a coyote a cat

Archy and Mehitabel are still plugging along valiantly, some-where in Arizona. Archy reports that the seven platinum-blonde kittens with which Mehitabel left Hollywood have now been reduced to two.

He adds:

> please tell me whether
> a coyote is of the cat family or not
> mehitabel has been very friendly lately
> with a coyote
> she says he has only a fatherly interest
> she said the same thing in Hollywood
> and then came the kittens
> the fifth one perished by the way
> while trying to get milk
> out of a cactus plant
> i asked mehitabel today if she were
> grieving for the other five
> and she replied what other five
> there is no doubt that mehitabel
> has suffered a good deal
> but one nice thing is that she does not
> seem to remember it long

xlviii

human nature aint that bad

A bulletin from Archy, who is back in New York and glad of
it.

thought i would never get home
did i tell you about the two bums
i listened to in california
named spike and cheesy
they were washing selves and clothes
in an irrigation ditch
cheesy says this valley was once the bottom
of the ocean dont that give you a queer feeling
now i know why i feel at home here says spike
my old man always said I would sink lower
than any other human on earth
and it appears that i have attained my goal at last
the long struggle of my life has ended
in complete victory i am finally at
where i was going to please pass the canned heat
i want to drink to the boy who made good
i suppose said cheesy we have been getting
a lot of handouts and nickels
really intended for workingmen out of jobs
never look a gift horse in the mouth said spike
but what I am afraid of said cheesy
is that this depression will end some time
and people will start offering me jobs again
cheer up said spike dont be a pessimist

we weathered lots of good times before
and we will manage to get through somehow
when they come again
you gotta look on the bright side of things
this depression is making the public gift minded
i dont know said cheesy i am scared
it will be just hell for me
when prosperity returns with an open job
on every four corners
listen said spike you are plain selfish
dont you know there are a lot of people
in this world who really like to work
cheesy took the canned heat and thought and thought
and thought and thought before he spoke again
i dont believe it he said finally
after all human nature aint that bad

archy

xlix

could such things be

A bulletin from Archy, who, with Mehitabel the Cat, started
out last July to hitch-hike from Hollywood to New York:

well boss here i am back in new york
i got a great break
after walking for months through arizona
i caught a ride on an airplane
and the first person i saw here was mehitabel
who had bummed her way
in a tourist trailer
she is living in shinbone alley
on second hand fish heads she drags away
from the east side markets
and she has some new kittens
they are the most peculiar kittens i ever saw
not the ones she left hollywood with
months ago or anything like them
there are five of these new ones
and they dont mew
they make a noise more like barking
i thought of that coyote she was so friendly with
in the southwest but i did not ask
any tactless questions
boss do you suppose such things could be

archy

1

be damned mother dear

Mehitabel the Cat is still living in Shinbone Alley with the strange kittens which arrived shortly after Mehitabel's arrival from the Southwest. Archy, the Cockroach, says . . . but let him tell it:

one of mehitabels kittens
licked a bull pup yesterday
and she is very proud
but hang them she says
i cant teach them to fight like cats
i told one of them yesterday
when i left home
i might bring him back
a pretty neck ribbon
if he was a good kitten
and he answered me in a strange voice
ribbon be damned mother dear
what i want is a brass collar
with spikes on it
and another one whom i had been
calling pussy says to me
pussy be damned mother dear
call me fido and another one
who got hold of a ball of catnip
complained it made him
sick at the stomach he says
catnip be damned mother dear

what i want is a bone to gnaw
what do you suppose makes them
act so strange archy
do you suppose i answered her
that prenatal influence
could have anything to do with it
perhaps that is it
she replied innocently
i seem to remember
that i was chased through
arizona and new mexico
by a coyote or did i dream
i will say you were chased
i told her my advice
is to rent them out
to a dog and pony show

archy

li

the artist always pays

boss i visited mehitabel last night
at her home in shinbone alley
she sat on a heap of frozen refuse
with those strange new kittens she has
frolicking around her
and sang a little song at the cold moon
which went like this

i have had my ups i have had my downs
i never was nobodys pet
i got a limp in my left hind leg
but theres life in the old dame yet

my first boy friend was a maltese tom
quite handsomely constructed
i trusted him but the first thing i knew
i was practically abducted

then i took up with a persian prince
a cat by no means plain
and that exotic son of a gun
abducted me again

what chance has an innocent kitten got
with the background of a lady

when feline blighters betray her trust
in ways lowlifed and shady

my next boy friend was a yellow bum
who loafed down by the docks
i rustled that gonifs rats for him
and he paid me with hard knocks

i have had my ups i have had my downs
i have led a helluva life
it was all these abductions unsettled my mind
for being somebodys wife

today i am here tomorrow flung
on a scow bound down the bay
but wotthehell o wotthehell
i m a lady thats toujours gai

my next boy friend was a theater cat
a kind of a backstage pet
he taught me to dance and get me right
theres a dance in the old dame yet

my next boy friend he left me flat
with a family and no milk
and i says to him as i lifted his eye
i ll learn ye how to bilk

i have had my ups i have had my downs
i have been through the mill
but in spite of a hundred abductions kid
i am a lady still

my next friend wore a ribbon and bells
but he laughed and left me broke
and i said as i sliced him into scraps
laugh off this little joke

some day my guts will be fiddle strings
but my ghost will dance while they play
for they cant take the pep from the old girls soul
and i am toujours gai

my heart has been broken a thousand times
i have had my downs and ups
but the queerest thing ever happened to me
is these kittens as turned out pups

o wotthehell o toujours gai
i never had time to fret
i danced to whatever tune was played
and theres life in the old dame yet

i have had my ups i have had my downs
i have been through the mill
but i said when i clawed that coyotes face
thank god i am a lady still

and then she added looking at those
extraordinary kittens of hers
archy i wish you would
take a little trip up to the zoo
and see if they have any department there
for odd sizes and new species

i got to find a home
for these damned freaks somewhere
poor little things my heart bleeds for them
it agonizes my maternal instinct
one way or another an artist always pays

　　　　archy

lii

maternal care

i was down in shinbone alley
yesterday on a visit
to mehitabel and her queer kittens
the ones which came
to her maternal care
after her journey through the southwest
damn them archy she said to me
i cant teach them to purr
and mew like kittens should
they only growl and bark
and yesterday the five of them
raided a butcher shop
around the corner and came home
with a whole lamb
and a cop chasing them
they turned on him
and tore half his clothes off of him
and he went away howling
that he would probably have
hydrophobia
archy they dont take after
any of my folks at all
i am beginning to think
they are a bunch of wild dogs
what have i ever done
to have these offspring wished on me
poor mehitabel

she gets such bad breaks
but wot the hell archy wot the hell
she says my motto is toujours gai
i may have made a false step or two
but i am always the lady
and theres a dance or two
in the old dame yet

archy

liii

to hell with anything common

well boss what should i see
last evening but our old friend
mehitabel the cat
she was finishing a fish head
she had dragged out of a garbage can
one of her eyes
was bloodshot but the other
glowed with the old
unconquerable lustre
there was a drab and ashen look
about her fur
but her step is swift and wiry
and her brave tail is still
a joyous banner in the air
has life been using you hard
mehitabel i asked her
pretty rough little cockroach
says she but what the hell
what the hell
toujours gai is my motto
always game and always gay
what the hell archy
theres a life or two
in the old girl yet i
am always jolly archy
am always the lady
what the hell

they cant take that away
from me archy
and always free archy
i live my own life archy
and i shall right up to the moment
the d s c wagon gets me
and carts me to the garbage scow
archy you may not believe it
but last week i received no less
than three offers of permanent homes
all from very respectable cats
with ribbons around their necks
but nothing doing
on this domesticity stuff
i am a free spirit
i am of royal descent archy
my grandmother was a persian
princess and i cant see myself
falling for any bourgeois
apartment house stuff
either a palace or else
complete liberty for me
i play a lone hand
and i never take up with tame toms
my particular friends have always
been very gentlemanly cats archy
to hell with anything common archy
that has always been my motto
always gay and always the lady
you cant trust half
of these damned pet cats
anyhow they will double cross
a lady with no conscience

only last week i was singing
on a back fence and one of these
dolled up johnnies came out of the basement
and joined me he had a silver bell on
kid he says to me i fall for you
why you sudden thing says i
i like your nerve
come live with me and be my love
says he and i will show you how
to pick open the ice box door
sweet thing says i
your line of talk convinces me
that we are affinities lead me to
the cream pitcher
i followed this slick crook
into the kitchen and just as we got
the ice box door open in came
the cook what does he do but pretend
he never knew me and she hits me
in the slats with a flat iron
was that any way to treat a lady
archy that cheap johnnie had
practically abducted me as you might say
and then deserted me
but what the hell archy what
the hell i am too much
the lady to beef about it
i laid for him in the alley
the next night and tore one of his
ears into fringes and lifted
an eye out of him now you
puzzle faced four flusher i told him
that will teach you how to

double cross a lady
always game and always gay
archy that is me what the hell
theres a dance or two
in the old dame yet
class is the thing that counts
archy you cant get away
from class

well boss i think that in spite
of her brave words and gallant
spirit our friend mehitabel
is feeling her years and constant
exposure to the elements
another year and i will likely
see her funeral cortege
winding through the traffic
a line of d s c wagons headed
for the refuse scows and poor
mehitabel ashily stark
in the foremost cart
                              archy

liv

a word from little archibald

thank you
for the mittens
socks and
muffler for me
knitted out of
frogs hair by one
of my admirers which
you so kindly
forwarded i suppose
the reason
i got them was that
they were too
small for you
to wear yourself
yours for rum
crime and riot

archy